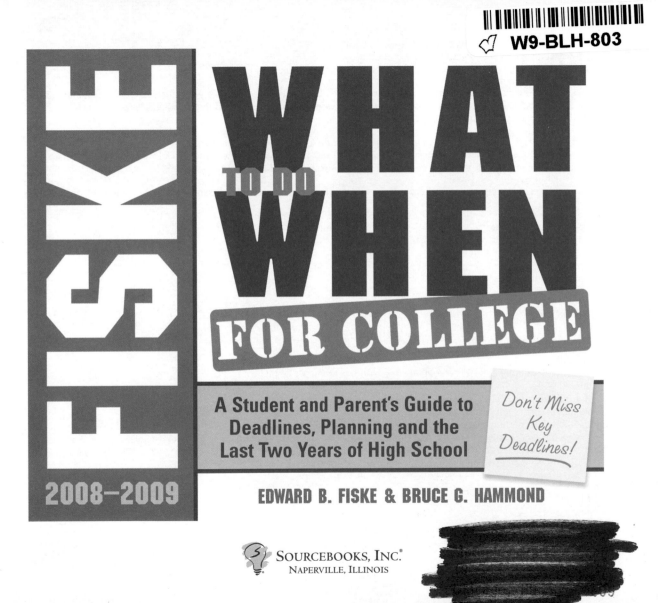

W9-BLH-803

FISKE

WHAT TO DO WHEN

FOR COLLEGE

A Student and Parent's Guide to
Deadlines, Planning and the
Last Two Years of High School

Don't Miss Key Deadlines!

2008–2009

EDWARD B. FISKE & BRUCE G. HAMMOND

SOURCEBOOKS, INC.
NAPERVILLE, ILLINOIS

Published by Sourcebooks, Inc.
P.O. Box 4410, Naperville, Illinois 60567–4410
(630) 961–3900
Fax: (630) 961–2168
www.sourcebooks.com

ISBN-13:978-1-4022-1047-1
ISBN-10:1-4022-1047-7

Previous edition cataloged as follows:

Fiske, Edward B.
    Fiske what to do when for college, 2008/2009 : a week-by-week guide / by Edward B. Fiske and Bruce G. Hammond.
        p. cm.
    Rev. ed. of: Fiske college deadline planner, 2004-2005. c2003.
    Includes index.
    ISDN 1-4022-0307-1 (alk. paper)
    1.   Universities and colleges--United States--Admission--Calendars. 2. High school students--Scholarships, fellowships, etc.-- United States--Calendars. 3. Deadlines--United States. I. Title: What to do when for college, 2005/2006. II. Hammond, Bruce G. III. Fiske, Edward B. Fiske college deadline planner, 2004-2005. IV. Title.

    LB2351.2.F565 2004
    378.1'61--dc22

2004024394

Printed and bound in the United States of America
DR 10 9 8 7 6 5 4 3 2 1

To Andrea

and Sunny

CONTENTS

How to Use This Book . . . . **ix**

Structure of the Book x

Take a Chill Pill, Mom and Dad . . . . **xi**

Keeping It All in Perspective xiii

For Parents: Things to Keep in Mind before Eleventh Grade . . . . **xv**

Let Your Child Make Choices xv

Don't Buy Your Child a Princeton Sweatshirt xv

The Pros and Cons of the National "Talent" Programs xvi

Picking the Right Courses xvii

High School Activities: Quality over Quantity xvii

The PSAT and PLAN xvii

Round One of the SAT xviii

The SAT Subject Tests xviii

Students with Disabilities: Testing and Documentation xix

Student's College Admission Pledge xx

Parent's College Admission Pledge xxi

Investigating the Academies xxii

January 2008 . . . . **1**

A Dose of Financial Reality 8

Summer in January 10

Congratulations! You're a Lucky Winner! 15

The Standardized Testing Money Machine 16

Hitting the Ground Running 17

February 2008 . . . . **19**

The National Merit Game 24

The Truth about Test Prep 25

College Essays: Window on the Soul or Just Plain Wacky? 31

Planning a Spring College Visit 32

Top Ten Signs that Mom and Dad Are Losing It 33

March 2008 . . . . **35**

    For Parents: Singin' Those Procrastination Blues 37

    Picking Courses for Twelfth Grade 39

    The SAT Gets a Makeover 42

    SAT and ACT: What's the Difference? 49

    Coming to Grips with Reality 51

April 2008 . . . . **53**

    What Flattery Will Get You 58

    Admission 101: The Big Picture 59

    How to Jump-Start the College Search 60

    The College Search in Cyberspace 61

    When Mom and Dad Run Amok: College Counselors Tell All 67

    A Pitch for Small Colleges 69

    The Long and Winding Road to an Athletic Scholarship 70

May–June 2008 . . . . **73**

    The APs: A Closer Look 78

    Thinking about Careers 79

    Prepping for the SAT Subject Tests 85

    Planning Summer Visits 86

    High School Courses versus Those at a Local College 87

    June 2008 88

    Top Five Pitfalls to a Successful College Visit 89

Summer 2008 . . . . **91**

    Summer for Free 92

September 2008 . . . . **97**

    The Annual Rankings Frenzy 101

    The Jefferson and Morehead Merit Scholarships 104

    The Early Game: To Play or Not to Play 105

    Cutting through Admission Office Double-Speak 110

    Rounding up Teacher Recommenders 111

    When Admission Officers Come to School 112

    For Parents: Top Five Signs of a Procrastination Emergency 113

October 2008 . . . . **115**

What's in an Application? 118

A Last Check of the Transcript 119

Inside the PSAT 120

For Parents: Another Chorus of Procrastination Blues 121

Ten Signs that the College Rat Race Is out of Control 128

November 2008 . . . . **129**

Essay Help: How Much Is Too Much? 133

The Application: Online versus Paper 136

College Essays Online: Another Moral Dilemma 137

The Common Application Conundrum 141

Combating Deer-in-the-Headlights Syndrome 142

Checking the List One More Time 143

December 2008 . . . . **145**

Sending Extra Material 152

Handling an Early Deferral or Denial 153

Top Five Myths of College Admission 154

Winter Break Deadline Emergency 155

What's in a Deadline? 155

Art Students Polish Their Portfolios 159

January 2009 . . . . **161**

"Your Application Is Incomplete" 166

Will I Be Competing against Others at My School? 167

Scholarships for Left-Handed Students? 173

How Admission Offices Really Work 174

February 2009 . . . . **175**

Is There a Prep School Advantage? 180

Surviving the Audition 181

Red Flags from the Admission Office 187

Appealing Directly to the Aid Office 188

"Wink Letters" Brighten February Spirits 189

March 2009 . . . . **191**

How Counselors Use Their Connections 193
Searching for Scholarships: The Local Angle. 195
What Has Gotten into You? Parents Want to Know 195
Taking a Year Off. 200
Living/Learning and Residential College Programs. 201
An Applicant's Worst Nightmare: Caught without a School 205

April–June 2009 . . . . **207**

The Nitty Gritty of Aid Awards. 210
Decisions, Decisions. 212
Some Acceptance Letters We'd Like to See (Translated for Parents) 213
Standardized Testing April–June 2009 216
Coping with the Waitlist 216
For Parents: The Summer before Leaving 218

A Note on the Appendices **221**

Appendix A: Standardized Tests **222**

SAT and Subject Tests Calendar—2008–2009 222
ACT Assessment Calendar—2008–2009 223
Colleges That Require SAT Subject Tests for Admission. 224
Colleges That Recommend SAT Subject Tests 225

Appendix B: Admission Deadlines **226**

Early-Decision Deadlines 226
Early-Action Deadlines 230
Regular Admission Deadlines 232

Appendix C: Scholarship Deadlines **237**

Independent Scholarships and Awards 237
General Interest Scholarships and Awards 237
Minority Interest Scholarships and Awards 239
Science and Technology-Related Scholarships and Awards 240
Essay Contests 241
Early-Bird Institutional Scholarships 242

Glossary **246**

Acknowledgments **249**

2008–2009 College Admission Calendar **251**

How to Use This Book

Deadlines, deadlines, deadlines. Life is full of them, but nowhere are deadlines more important than in college admission. The story is the same whether you're applying for admission, registering for standardized tests, or trying to win a scholarship: Find out the due date and get it there on time.

The main purpose of *Fiske What to Do When for College* is to help families stay on top of the welter of deadlines in college admission. The book follows key dates in the admission process week-by-week, but we recommend that you read it long before the crucial dates arrive. Meeting any deadline typically requires plenty of advance preparation.

Because the calendar is so crucial in college admission, we have built the entire book around dates and deadlines. We cover the process month-by-month and week-by-week from January 2008 through early April of 2009. The dates in this book are all national deadlines that fall mainly into several categories:

- **Standardized testing.** We have included the registration deadlines, late-registration deadlines, and test dates for the SAT and ACT through the spring of 2009. Most of these dates have already been announced by the test-makers.

- **Application deadlines.** Included are early-decision, early-action, regular-decision, and financial aid deadlines at major institutions. All such deadlines, unless otherwise noted, are for students in twelfth grade.

- **Institutional scholarship deadlines.** Many colleges have early deadlines for their major scholarships. We have listed all institutional scholarship deadlines at major institutions. Unless otherwise noted, scholarships are for current twelfth graders and are renewable for four years.

- **Portable scholarship and contest deadlines.** Private corporations and foundations offer portable scholarships and awards. They are portable because they can be used at any college. Unless otherwise noted, scholarships and contests are for twelfth graders.

Many of the dates, such as those for SAT and ACT testing, have already been announced through spring of 2009. Other dates, such as scholarship and admission deadlines, are subject to change. Therefore, **we recommend that you verify all admission and scholarship dates with the appropriate authority.** Where possible, the book includes Web links to allow you to do so with a few quick clicks.

> I wish I had started earlier with the whole college search process. It comes up quickly.
>
> —University of Michigan student

Various parts of the book will be more or less useful depending on whether you are in the Class of 2008, the Class of 2009, or a future class. In the winter and early spring, the application and scholarship deadlines generally apply to twelfth graders, while testing deadlines generally apply to eleventh graders. In the fall, most deadlines apply to twelfth graders. In general, scholarship competitions are available to twelfth graders only, while essay contests, science fairs, and other competitions with cash awards may be open to younger students.

Structure of the Book

The structure of this book is user-friendly and easy to follow. The format consists of the following:

Monthly overviews. These consist of brief summaries of the month's priorities, including a list of key dates called "What To Do." Use these dates as a quick guide to the most important stuff.

Weekly Calendar entries. This is your practical guide to the nuts and bolts of college planning, including details about scholarship programs, admission deadlines, testing deadlines, and every other date you can think of.

The Daily Planner. Every date through April of 2009 is listed. Use this as your college admission calendar. We hope that you will record your own personal appointments and due dates alongside those that are listed.

Advice Essays. Along with our What To Do commentary, we offer additional essays about various facets of the admission process. From planning college visits to prepping for the SAT, these include our best advice for every facet of the college search. We have placed these essays adjacent to the weeks and months of the calendar when the advice is most timely.

Quotes from Students, Parents, and Counselors. As part of our research for this book, we surveyed more than two hundred students and dozens of parents and counselors. The best of their advice is included in the bold quotations spread throughout the text. We chose "Counselor's heads-up" to denote advice from the guidance office, and to ensure the candor of our sources, we made these quotations anonymous. We identify students and parents by where they (or their sons and daughters) decided to attend college.

Appendices. What, you may ask, are appendices? The short answer is that the word "appendices" is the plural of appendix, which is a section that includes information that supplements the regular text. (Our hearty congratulations if you already knew all that.) Our appendices include lists of all the important dates in the book by category—SAT

dates, ACT dates, admission and scholarship deadlines, and much more. For a complete list of what you'll find in the appendices, turn to the main contents or the mini contents on page 221.

> I've learned the hard way that a good essay and solid test scores can't always make up for a mediocre GPA.
>
> —Lewis & Clark College student

Since we know that the admission process is stressful, we have included a few additional items to lighten the mood. We hope you will enjoy the Student and Parent Pledges on pages xx and xxi as a light-hearted but serious reminder to keep both feet on the ground. With apologies to David Letterman, we also offer a few Top Five and Top Ten lists that we hope will both amuse and enlighten you.

TAKE A CHILL PILL, MOM AND DAD

This book is designed to be the savviest one yet on the nuts and bolts of getting into college. Our primary audience is eleventh and twelfth graders—with maybe a few on-the-ball tenth graders mixed in. We hope you will read through the book at the

beginning of your college search, and then refer to it again and again as key deadlines near.

We also hope that this book will be useful to parents, and we address many passages directly to them. Why include mom and dad? Let's do a reality check. Which person in your household is the one who reminds everyone else about approaching deadlines, who plans ahead months (or years) for every phase of the college search? If any students out there are nodding and pointing to themselves, we invite you to grab this book and get started. You have our permission to cut Mom and Dad out of the loop—with maybe an occasional update and some consultation about finances.

We're betting that most households work in a slightly different way, and we're not ready to put Mom and Dad out to pasture just yet. In most families, parents play an important role in the admission process. Parents, the balance is delicate: How can you grease the wheels without gumming up the works? Or, to change the metaphor, how can you pave the way without dictating the path? As long as you remember the fundamental truth about the college search—that it's all about the students—you can play a productive and even crucial role.

Letting go is hard, and it begins before the first college viewbook hits the mailbox. For parents accustomed to making decisions on behalf of their children, the college search is a new phase of life. Haltingly at first, but with growing confidence, students can emerge from the shadow of Mom and Dad as the process unfolds. Some parents think

that because college is so important, they need to step in. When parents feel that urge coming on, the right response is often to step back.

> **Consider colleges that you've never heard of, including those with funny names.**
>
> **—Counselor's heads-up**

For students and parents alike, we offer the unvarnished truth about the college search—day-by-day, week-by-week. But keep this in mind: No college search will ever happen exactly on the timetable outlined here. Just because we cover it day-by-day does not mean you should be stressing about it day-by-day. Different dates will be relevant to different students. Use this book as a guideline, not as a blueprint for when everything must take place.

We are concerned that in many schools and many families, the college search has spun out of control. The pressures on today's applicants would have been unimaginable twenty years ago. From every corner of a student's universe, the message comes loud and clear that self-worth is synonymous with high SAT scores and college acceptance letters:

- High schools measure their own worth by which colleges their students get into and how many of these students have high test scores.

- Colleges tout themselves based on their selectivity and on the test scores and class rank of their entering class.

- Parents (some of them, anyway) act as if they will accept nothing less than a "name" school acceptable in their social circles.

High school students are not stupid. They absorb all these messages while the stakes keep getting higher. Meanwhile, admission gets tougher and tougher as the Baby Boom echo continues to work its way through the school system.

Compassionate parents must fight a guerrilla campaign against the idea that intellectual ability (and college admission) equals self-worth. Parents should praise their sons and daughters for something other than A's on the report card. Keep an open mind about colleges you may not have heard of. Teenagers should have the space to be teenagers. Assure them that wherever they choose go to college will be just fine.

Keeping It All in Perspective

The hysteria surrounding admission to the nation's most selective colleges has reached scary proportions. What is behind it? Some parents swear that getting into a prestigious college means a fast track to a plum job, a great career, and a rewarding life. The theory is interesting, but there is no evidence to support it. Undeniably, a high-brow diploma comes in handy in a student's first job interview. After that, one's alma mater doesn't mean much outside the cocktail party circuit.

Do lesser-known institutions have any advantages? You bet they do. Let's say a top student turns down Stanford and goes to Lawrence University in Appleton, Wisconsin, or enrolls in the honors program at Ohio University. Top students at places such as these will get some or all of the following:

- A merit scholarship

- Small classes with top faculty

- Research opportunities normally reserved for graduate students

> **My son was reluctant to go on college visits and almost had to be dragged to the schools we saw.**
>
> **—Lehigh University mom**

- First shot at special summer opportunities

- Grooming for postgraduate fellowships

- Great graduate school recommendations from professors who really know them

- The satisfaction of being near the top rather than in the middle of the pack

Good luck on getting all this at Prestige U as another face in the glossy crowd.

> **Picking a college doesn't have to be voodoo. There are 2,200 four-year colleges in the country, and about 200 of them will be "right" for a student.**
>
> **—Counselor's heads-up**

We realize that many students will still want to play the highly selective college game. As graduates of Wesleyan and Yale, we will not try to dissuade anyone. Four years at a highly selective college can be an incredible experience for the right student. But the highly selective hysteria is not about having a good experience, getting a good education, or finding the right job. Rather, it is about recognition, self-image, and joining an exclusive club. There is nothing wrong with seeking distinction—everyone does it. But let's be honest with ourselves about what is really at stake.

As the book unfolds, we poke fun at the hyper-anxiety that has taken over the college search. To keep pedantic lecturing to a minimum, we have summarized some of our most crucial themes in the Student's and Parent's College Admission Pledges that follow on pages xx and xxi. We hope you will laugh as you see a bit of yourself in our caricatures. We also hope families will read these together and discuss the themes we raise. The tone is lighthearted, but our message for parents is consistent: Keep your eye firmly on what is best for your son or daughter's long-term well-being.

There are a lot of desperately unhappy students enrolled at the Harvards of the world, and many more who are on their way to a happy and successful life attending colleges few people have ever heard of. Some students think that a void in their lives will be filled by a prestigious alma mater. They are sadly mistaken. What today's students really need is the absolute certainty that their parents will love and respect them no matter where they go to college. We urge students to look inside themselves for the qualities that do not depend on the verdict of an admission committee. It is those qualities, not an acceptance letter, that will sustain them as they go forward to begin a new stage in their life.

For Parents: Things to Keep in Mind before Eleventh Grade

The college search often starts early—sometimes a little too early:

- A pregnant mother calls the local private school to put her son-to-be on the waiting list.

- The father of a two-year-old phones Harvard and Yale to find out the preferred preschool in his city for grooming an Ivy Leaguer.

- Parents pay hundreds of dollars for a consultant to coach their four-year-old for the high-stakes prekindergarten interview that will determine admission to primary school.

Although the rest of the country may roll its eyes, anecdotes like this are commonplace in Boston, New York, and other East Coast cities. Everybody is chasing the same prize, and the race starts early. There is nothing wrong with being ambitious, but we counsel parents to temper the stresses whenever possible.

Most parents reading this book have kids of high school age, but some of you may be planning ahead for younger ones. The following is a brief survey of dos and don'ts through the winter of eleventh grade. (Students should feel free to skip down to "Picking the Right Courses.")

Let Your Child Make Choices

Any good kindergarten teacher will tell you that children learn best in a stimulating environment where they are free to pursue their interests. The same applies to preparation for college. Parents do more harm than good when they try to mold their children into a preconceived notion of well-roundedness. Admission offices prefer students who are exceptionally good in one or two activities rather than reasonably good in ten. A detailed regimen of the "right" activities will only succeed in making your son or daughter just like everyone else's. Broad exposure is important, but so too is the freedom to pursue a few strong interests.

Don't Buy Your Child a Princeton Sweatshirt

Or, if your son or daughter already has a Princeton sweatshirt, find a place to tuck it away. Such things may seem innocent, but they carry a subtle message. The danger is most acute when Mom and Dad graduated from prestigious alma maters. Fewer than half of the high school valedictorians who apply to Princeton are admitted; how sad when preteens are saddled with those expectations. Many colleges now receive twice as many applications as they did in the 1980s, and even the adults who attended prestigious schools back then might not be admitted today. Even if your alma mater is not highly selective, tread lightly. Push too hard and your son or daughter just might push back.

> Help your child find the right fit: Not your alma mater, not their friends' choice, but the place best suited to him or her.
>
> —Amherst College dad

The Pros and Cons of the National "Talent" Programs

The best-known national academic programs for elementary and middle schoolers are the self-styled "talent programs": the Center for Talented Youth at Johns Hopkins University (www.cty.jhu.edu); the Talent Identification Program at Duke University (www.tip.duke.edu); the Center for Talent Development at Northwestern University (www.ctd.northwestern.edu); and the Rocky Mountain Talent Search at the University of Denver (www.du.edu/education/ces/rmts.html). These organizations divide the country regionally and offer enrichment programs for students through the elementary, middle, and early high school years. The talent programs identify potential applicants based on high test scores on school-administered standardized tests. Beginning in seventh grade, these programs give students the option of taking the SAT in order to qualify. Successful students earn recognition and attend summer programs on the campuses of the respective universities. Some critics argue that the talent programs introduce college-style pressure and competition to the middle grades, and that the SAT is better saved until high school. But some students say that taking the SAT at an early age helps raise their comfort level when they see it again in later years. As to the experience that these programs offer, most attendees give them a thumbs-up.

Picking the Right Courses

No matter what their age, students should take appropriately challenging courses—with an emphasis on the word "appropriately." Mental health (and grade point average) can suffer when students are overloaded. Under most circumstances, students should take a course every year in the core areas of English, history, math, science, and foreign language. But some students may not be cut out to take the honors track in every subject, or may want to devote more energy to arts or computer courses instead of taking Honors French III. A common parental mistake is to try to shoehorn their kids into the accelerated math track, often against the school's advice. If C's are the result, it won't help. For a peek ahead at what colleges look for in a high school curriculum, consult their websites or publications. For advice on picking courses for grade twelve, see page 39.

High School Activities: Quality over Quantity

Some high school students have the idea that sitting in the back of a few SADD meetings or getting inducted into the National Honor Society will make their college application stand out. Not so. Extracurricular activities and jobs are valuable when they show one of the following: initiative, passion, leadership, or distinction. Unusual talents or activities are more interesting than run-of-the-mill ones, but don't count on a community service project in Kashmir to be the magic bullet. Colleges recognize that wealthy families have better access to fancy-schmancy programs in faraway places. Compelling qualities can also be shown close to home. Our advice to students: Do what you love, and stick with it.

I have actually had a college call me and say, "Get your parents off of the phone!" If the parents call, the colleges immediately assume that the student is too lazy or stupid to pick up the phone and dial ten numbers.

—Counselor's heads-up

The PSAT and PLAN

Many high schools administer the Preliminary SAT to students in October of tenth grade. Some schools also administer the PLAN, a pre-ACT, generally in the fall of tenth grade. In eleventh grade, the vast majority of high schools administer the PSAT, and this time high scorers are eligible for recognition in the National Merit

Scholarship Program. (For details, see page 24.) Check with your guidance counselor to see when these tests are offered. If a school does not offer one or the other, students may arrange to take the test(s) at a school that does. These tests are valuable because they can help predict a student's SAT and ACT scores and help determine which one will offer them the best chance of scoring high. Families can also use scores from the PSAT or PLAN as a basis for considering an SAT or ACT prep course.

> It was hard not to nag in the beginning when I felt my son should be doing more. We gave him our suggestions for schools and topics for essays, but then had to step back and let him make the decisions.
>
> —Harvey Mudd College mom

Round One of the SAT

Among high school counselors, talking about the SAT for students younger than eleventh grade is a little like talking about bad breath. *Eeesh.* Nobody wants to feed the hype that is already rampant, or turn top students into stressed-out SAT weenies. But preparing for and/or taking the SAT in tenth grade may make sense for a few of the most advanced students. First, the math section of the SAT covers material that top students typically learn in ninth or tenth grade. When such students are questioned about taking the SAT, many say they suffered from being rusty on the math. Second, tenth grade is generally less stressful than eleventh, giving motivated students the time and energy to focus on the test. Last, strong students with a good shot at National Merit honors will probably want to do their prepping before taking the PSAT in October of eleventh grade. An SAT in May or June of tenth grade could make sense for some accelerated students, as could some prep for the SAT or PSAT in the summer after tenth grade. (For more on prep courses, see page 15.)

The SAT Subject Tests

SAT Subject Tests are hour-long tests in subjects such as writing, U.S. history, math, the sciences, and foreign language, twenty-one of them all told. SAT Subject Tests are required or recommended by a few dozen of the nation's most selective institutions. (For a complete list, see Appendix A.) Most students take the SAT Subject Tests beginning in June of eleventh grade, but an increasing number of early birds take them in tenth and even ninth grade. Such students are looking for an early read on how they can score, and want to reduce the pressure on themselves in eleventh grade. The Subject Tests are generally best taken at the end of a school year, after students have covered the material and while it is still fresh. Some intrepid ninth graders take the biology test, and chemistry is a likely choice for tenth graders. Accelerated math students taking precalculus or the equivalent in tenth grade may want to try the Math Level II exam. We recommend that only exceptionally strong students attempt subject tests before eleventh grade. Keep in mind that all Subject Test scores are part of the student's testing record and will be reported to all colleges they apply to.

Students with Disabilities: Testing and Documentation

Students with physical and learning disabilities have the right to take college admission tests with appropriate accommodations, including extended time, large print, an audio version of the test, and so on. The scores of tests taken with accommodations such as these are no longer "flagged," so students should not hesitate. Schools file the paperwork, and the test-makers have two basic requirements for nonstandard testing:

- A diagnostic evaluation of the student and recommendation for extended time on the test by a qualified professional

- Evidence that the school has acknowledged the disability and is granting similar accommodations for that student in class

Families should initiate the approval process as soon as possible and no later than the beginning of tenth grade. Both the College Board and the ACT require diagnostic testing within the preceding three years to confirm the original evaluation. Both are also finicky about approving accommodations for students whose initial diagnosis comes within the context of the college admission process. If you've ever wondered about testing your child, do it sooner rather than later.

> The flood of mail tends to make students think they are being sought after—and they may be—or maybe they are just being encouraged to apply to increase the application numbers.
>
> —Counselor's heads-up

Student's College Admission Pledge

I have accepted the fact that my parents are clueless. I am serene. I will not bat an eyelash when they offer opinions or advice, no matter how laughable. My soul will be light as a feather when my mother elbows her way to the front of my college tour and talks the guide's ear off. I am serene.

Going to college is a stressful time for my parents, even though they are not the ones going. I recognize that neurosis is beyond anyone's control. Each week, I will calmly reassure them that I am working on my essays, have registered for my tests, am finishing my applications, have scheduled my interviews, am aware of all deadlines, and will have everything done in plenty of time. I will smile good-naturedly as my parent asks four follow-up questions at College Night.

I will try not to say no simply because my parents say yes, and remain open to the possibility, however improbable, that they may have a point. I may not be fully conscious of my anxieties about the college search—the fear of being judged and the fear of leaving home are both strong. I don't really want to leave high school as much as I say I do, and it is easier to put off the college search than it is to get it done. My parents are right about the importance of being proactive, even if they do get carried away.

Although the college search belongs to me, I pledge to listen to my parents. They know me better than anyone else, and they are the ones who will pay most of the bills. Their ideas about what is best for me are based on years of experience in the real world. I will seriously consider what they say as I form my own opinions.

I must take charge of the college search. If I do, the nagging will stop and everyone's anxiety will go down. My parents have given me a remarkable gift—the ability to think and do for myself. I know I can do it with a little help from Mom and Dad.

Parent's College Admission Pledge

I am resigned to the fact that my child's college search will end in disaster. I am serene. Deadlines will be missed and scholarships will be lost as my child lounges under pulsating headphones or stares transfixed at an X-box. I accept the fact that I am a parent and therefore know nothing. I am serene.

Confronted with endless procrastination, my impulse is to take control—to register for tests, plan visits, schedule interviews, and get applications. It was I who asked those four follow-up questions at College Night—I couldn't help myself. And yet I know that everything will be fine if I can summon the fortitude to relax. My child is smart, capable, and perhaps a little too accustomed to me jumping in and fixing things. I will hold back. I pledge to drop hints and encourage, then back off. I will facilitate rather than dominate. The college search won't happen on my schedule, but it will happen.

I will not get too high or low about any facet of the college search. Were I to do so, I would give it more importance than it really has. My child's self-worth may already be too wrapped up in getting an acceptance letter. I will attempt to lessen the fear rather than heighten it.

I will try not to say no simply because my son or daughter says yes, and I will remain open to the possibility, however improbable, that my child has the most important things under control. I understand that my anxiety comes partly from a sense of impending loss. I can feel my child slipping away. Sometimes I hold on too tightly or let social acceptability cloud the issue of what is best.

I realize that my child is almost ready to go and that a little rebellion at this time of life can be a good thing. I will respect and encourage independence, even if some of it is expressed as resentment toward me. I will make suggestions with care and try to avoid unnecessary confrontation.

Paying for college is my responsibility. I will take a major role in the search for financial aid and scholarships and speak honestly to my child about the financial realities we face.

I pledge to help my son or daughter take charge of the college search. I will try to support but not smother, encourage but not annoy, and consult but not control. The college search is too big to be handled alone—I will be there every step of the way.

Investigating the Academies

This applies only to students who think they may be cut out for attending the Army, Navy, Air Force, Coast Guard, or Merchant Marine academies. Interested students should begin exploring this option by the fall of eleventh grade. Candidates must generally be nominated to the academies by members of Congress, many of whom hold information nights for prospective students in the fall. Contact the office of your senator or representative. Application deadlines vary. Candidates are evaluated on the basis of academic achievement, leadership, and physical fitness. Interested students should consider attending one of the week-long summer programs held at the academies for a taste of the military lifestyle. (See noteworthy summer programs, page 91.)

> As long as I didn't mention my favorite school, my daughter would listen to me. But my personal favorite was completely rejected.
>
> —Tufts University mom

> I realized that the paperwork was a formidable task for a busy high school senior, and agreed to organize the process in terms of files, deadlines, and dealing with the volumes of mail.
>
> —Yale University mom

It is important to lay the groundwork for a successful college search, but high school should not be reduced to a cram session for college. Too many teens arrive at college as burned-out survivors rather than eager learners. If thoughts of planning for college are dominating your life—or if your teen is showing signs of college stress—find ways to ease the tension and bring back a little joy.

Sometimes the best antidote for anxiety is information. The pages that follow detail all the twists and turns in the college admission process, week-by-week. For an extended discussion of the topics herein, pick up a copy of the *Fiske Guide to Getting into the Right College.*

JANUARY 2008

FOR THE CLASS OF **2008,** regular-decision deadlines come thick and fast this month. Financial aid applications should be filed by the end of January. Students who have been knee-deep in the admission process can use this month to refocus on the scholarship search.

Eleventh graders should begin their college search in earnest this month and plan for visits over spring break. Now is also the time to think about a standardized test schedule for the spring. What combination of SAT, ACT, and the Subject Tests will you take? (For advice, see pages 49 and 85.) January is also a good time to give serious thought to summer travel plans.

WHAT TO DO:

✓ **Tuesday, January 1**
Regular-decision deadlines at the most selective colleges

✓ **Tuesday, January 15**
Regular-decision deadlines at highly selective colleges

✓ **Saturday, January 26**
SAT and Subject Tests administered

✓ **Tuesday, January 29**
March SAT registration deadline

January 1–5, 2008

For the Class of 2008, the new year brings a rush to the post office for last-minute applicants to highly selective colleges. January 1 is the admission deadline at all eight of the Ivy League universities; at little Ivies such as **Amherst, Williams, Wesleyan,** and **Swarthmore;** and at the likes of **MIT, Caltech, Bucknell, Duke,** and **Northwestern,** to name a few. (With no mail service on New Year's Day, "January 1" really means "December 31," though some schools, **Columbia** and **Caltech** among them, officially give students until January 2.) Early Decision (ED) II, a second round of binding commitment ED deadlines after those in November, arrives at places such as **Bates, Emory, Hobart and William Smith, Scripps,** and **Swarthmore.** (For a complete list of January 1 deadlines, see Appendix B.) A small smattering of other colleges have deadlines scattered through the first week of January.

January 1 is the first day that the FAFSA can be legally filed for students entering college in the fall of 2008. Chase down those W-2's and 1099's as fast as possible. For families who plan to file the FAFSA online, both student and parent should secure a PIN for their electronic signature as soon as possible at www.pin.ed.gov.

Most eleventh graders are dimly aware that they will one day go to college, and February is generally a good time for a first crack at the ACT. Students can then take the test a second time in April or June to have two scores in time for a possible early-decision or early-action application. The first fall date available nationwide is in October, and while scores generally arrive in time for early consideration, you may not see them before the deadline.

The **United Nations Association National High School Essay Contest** offers three awards of up to $3,000 and is open to students in grades 9–12.

Tuesday, January 1

- ☐ Application deadlines at the most selective colleges
- ☐ Early Decision II deadlines

_____

_____

- ☐ Institutional scholarship deadlines
- ☐ First day to file the Free Application for Federal Student Aid (FAFSA) for 2008–2009. www.fafsa.ed.gov

_____

Wednesday, January 2

- ☐ United Nations Association National High School Essay Contest. www.unausa.org

_____

_____

Thursday, January 3

- ☐ Bennington College and Vanderbilt University, application deadline

_____

_____

Friday, January 4

- ☐ February ACT registration deadline
- ☐ January SAT late-registration deadline

_____

Saturday, January 5

- ☐ Emerson College, admission deadline

_____

_____

January 6–12, 2008

January 15 has traditionally been the second date circled in red on the calendar of regular-decision deadlines, but a growing number of institutions now use January 10. The January 10 list includes **Elon, Georgetown, George Washington, Occidental,** and **University of Southern California.**

Seniors should seek out their guidance counselors to make sure that transcripts and recommendations have been forwarded to all colleges. Midyear grades will be sent in the next several weeks, and students should alert their counselors to any new awards or other information that could be included in the report (such as your recent selection to the all-district volleyball team). In cases where you have personally met an admission officer (AO), it would be a nice touch to send an email letting the AO know that the application is on its way.

The nation's premier scholarship for minority students—the **Gates Millennium**—offers more than one thousand renewable full-ride scholarships to those with high financial need. The **Ron Brown Scholar Program**, with a deadline of January 9, is the nation's most competitive for African Americans. In a recent year, there were 8,500 applications for the twenty scholarships offering a four-year total of $40,000. The **Elks MVS** offers five hundred renewable awards of up to $15,000 per year, and financial need is a factor. For raw numbers of scholarships, the **Sam Walton Community Scholarship** (of Wal-Mart fame) is probably the nation's largest, offering more than six thousand one-time awards of up to $25,000. Local winners have the chance to continue in the competition for scholarships totaling $25,000.

For eleventh graders, the first two weeks of January is the traditional time for a school-sponsored College Night to kick off or continue the college search. Mom sits in the front row, feverishly taking notes and asking questions; you sit in the back, giggling with friends and sinking lower in your seat every time Mom's hand goes up. So much for College Search 101.

The **Telluride Association** sponsors two of the nation's elite summer programs in the humanities. A program for eleventh graders (deadline late January) is open to all, while one for tenth-graders is open to minority students. Both are free. The **JFK Profile in Courage Essay Contest** offers one-time scholarships of up to $3,000 to students in grades 9–12.

Sunday, January 6

_____

_____

_____

_____

Monday, January 7

☐ Villanova University and Santa Clara University, admission deadline

Tuesday, January 8

☐ Millsaps College, early action deadline

_____

Wednesday, January 9

☐ Ron Brown Scholar Program. African Americans. www.ronbrown.org

Thursday, January 10

☐ Application deadlines at highly selective colleges

_____

Friday, January 11

☐ Elks Most Valuable Student Scholarship. www.elks.org/enf/scholars/mvs.cfm

☐ Gates Millenium Scholarship. www.gmsp.org

☐ Telluride Association Summer Programs, 10th Grade. www.tellurideassociation.org

☐ Sam Walton Community Scholarship. www.walmartfoundation.org

Saturday, January 12

☐ JFK Profile in Courage Essay Contest. www.jfklibrary.org

_____

JANUARY 13–19, 2008

The hit parade of highly selective colleges with January 15 admission deadlines includes **Colorado College, Emory, New York University, Oberlin, Reed,** and many more. Early Decision (ED) II, a second round of binding-commitment deadlines, is mainly the domain of small private colleges. Among those with January 15 ED II deadlines are **Carleton, Colgate, Drew, Skidmore,** and **Wheaton (MA).**

The intensely competitive **National Honor Society** (NHS) scholarship offers state, regional, and national awards totaling $200,000. A school nomination is required.

In the middle of January, summer vacation can seem light-years away to a stressed-out eleventh grader—good thing Mom and Dad are there for a gentle reminder. Now is the time to think seriously about summer.

Sunday, January 13

_____   _____

_____   _____

_____   _____

Monday, January 14

_____   _____

_____   _____

_____   _____

Tuesday, January 15

☐ Application deadlines at highly selective colleges
☐ Early Decision II deadlines at moderately selective colleges

_____

Wednesday, January 16

_____

_____

_____

Thursday, January 17

_____

_____

_____

Friday, January 18

☐ February ACT late-registration deadline
☐ National Honor Society Scholarship. www.naassp.org

Saturday, January 19

If your college fund is in tatters and finding a spare $150,000 is not an option, get set for a dose of reality. You may not be able to afford your dream school. Twenty years ago, we would have told you to take a deep breath and wait for the need-based aid. But with tuition up, grants down, and middle-income families feeling the heat, the financial bottom line cannot be ignored.

> I believe that students should have a certain arrogance when applying to colleges—meaning that you should have confidence in what you've done in your previous three years and know that whatever happens, happens.
>
> —Duke University student

Is Dream U out of reach? It is too early to know in January of eleventh grade, but this month is a perfect time for families to sit down and go over the financial parameters of the college search. Do it now—before anybody gets his or her heart set on a school that may not be realistic.

Some parents hem and haw, avoid the issue, and then pull the rug out in April of twelfth grade. Parents, the time is now to put your cards on the table—just because you may not be able to afford some colleges doesn't make you a bad parent. Expensive is not always better. Have a candid conversation about the role that finances may play. Don't eliminate Dream U—you never know what scholarships or aid may come down the pike—but help your child hedge his or her bets by identifying options that are likely to be less expensive. Here are some strategies:

- **Investigate need-based aid.** Go to www.collegeboard.com and click on "Paying for College" and then "How Much Will Your Family Have to Pay?" There, you'll find a program that will estimate your ability to qualify for aid. Better still, go ahead and file this year's Free Application for Federal Student Aid (FAFSA) even though your student is only an eleventh grader. You won't actually get money because your child will still be in high school in 2007–2008, but the report you get back will tell you how much you would be expected to pay for college.

• **Target a Merit Scholarship.** Encourage your son or daughter to identify schools where a merit scholarship might be in the cards. The best bet: colleges where the student would rank high in the applicant pool. A merit scholarship search can uncover gems that offer the benefits of being a big fish in a small pond.

Always fill out the information cards even if you know you are already on the college's mailing list. Never miss an opportunity to get an official "contact" in the computer system.

—Counselor's heads-up

• **Look for Bargains.** Every year, the *Fiske Guide to Colleges* lists the nation's best bargains, and the *Fiske Guide to Getting into the Right College* has a guide to budget options. In-state colleges are generally less expensive, and many states have reciprocity agreements with institutions in neighboring states. As an example, students in thirteen Western states can get reduced tuition at participating institutions in the other states under the Western Undergraduate Exchange.

The final decision of where to go should always belong to the student. Though parents may set financial limits, there are many outstanding colleges within any reasonable economic parameters.

Which summer activities look good on a college application? The kind where students can show initiative and independence while furthering an interest that will be reinforced by other parts of their application. Page one of the standard playbook is a summer program at a college or university. A summer on campus is a dry run for the real thing. Students get to sample dorm life, interact with real professors, and learn the importance of time management. The major negative to summer study is that students don't get a break from academics. Worst-case scenario, students will go straight from their summer exams to the beginning of regular school.

Many people overestimate the extent to which a summer on campus will give students a leg up in the regular admission process. Colleges use summer programs to make money from facilities that would otherwise be idle. As long as the family is forking over $1,000-plus per week, they are not overly picky about who gets in. Even Harvard will admit almost any student with good grades and supportive recommendations. Going to a university summer program won't mean much in the real admission process, with the following exceptions:

- The student has middling grades and uses the summer to show that he or she is capable of college-level work.

- The student works closely with a professor who can write a strong letter of recommendation.

One other option that can cost a pretty penny is summer abroad. It can be a great opportunity, especially when you are reinforcing language skills or other interests. Better still: a summer of service abroad with programs such as Amigos de las Americas (www.amigoslink.org) or

> I found that I was talking too much about the college process and adding stress to an already stressful situation. Once I stepped back and let my daughter take charge, things went more smoothly.
>
> —Knox College mom

The Experiment in International Living (www.usexperiment.org).

While a big-money summer program can be a great experience, there are plenty of other worthy options that won't cost the equivalent of a year's tuition at a state university. They include:

- Volunteer work
- Employment, preferably with the chance for leadership and responsibility
- An internship, paying or nonpaying, in a profession of interest

When in doubt, remember: initiative and independence. Better to start something than plug into somebody else's program, and better to show some imagination than follow the well-worn path.

> Girls are getting the shaft in college admission because of the imbalance of males to females on many college campuses. This is an important issue that no one is discussing openly.
>
> —Counselor's heads-up

January 20–26, 2008

January is the time for eleventh graders to get serious about their testing schedules. A few early birds will have already taken an SAT in the fall, but we recommend that ambitious students consider their first SAT in either January or March with a second round in May or June. If this planner had started in December, we would have noted that December 26 was the registration deadline for the SAT on January 26. For an extra $37, students who have not registered in advance can take the test as a standby by simply showing up at a test center with a completed registration form and a check in hand. Some test centers run out of room, so consult the College Board's list of centers, choose a likely one, and call the testing coordinator early in the week of the test to find out if they will have space. Standbys are always the last to get seated, but the process usually works.

The deadline for the **Telluride Association's** prestigious summer program for eleventh graders is this week. Open to students in grades 7–12, the **DuPont Challenge** requires an essay of not more than one thousand words on a scientific topic for one-time scholarships up to $5,000.

Sunday, January 20

☐ Grinnell College and University of Maryland admissions deadlines

Monday, January 21

Tuesday, January 22

Wednesday, January 23

Thursday, January 24

Friday, January 25

☐ DuPont Challenge Essay Contest.
www.glcomm/dupont

☐ Telluride Association Summer Program, 11th graders.
www.tellurideassociation.org

Saturday, January 26

☐ SAT and Subject Tests administered

January 27–31, 2008

The days of January typically find the parents of twelfth graders pulling their hair out at www.fafsa.ed.gov. In the early days of the Internet, the site was a disaster of lost data, broken links, and endless waiting for pages to load. Many of the bugs have been fixed (knock on wood) and filing the FAFSA online is now required. Ideally, you'll file on the basis of a completed 2007 tax form. In the real world, many parents file the FAFSA (and CSS PROFILE) on the basis of estimated income figures. On the downside, filing on estimates increases the likelihood that you will be selected for verification—the equivalent of an audit. Plus, if you are off by more than $400 in your estimates, you'll need to file a correction.

The **Discover Card Tribute Award** is one of the few recognition programs targeted solely at eleventh graders and is among the nation's most competitive, with nearly five hundred one-time awards of up to $25,000. **Miami of Ohio** chooses to live on the edge with a January 31 application deadline—as opposed to the more conventional February 1. **Toshiba** teams up with the **National Science Teachers Association** to offer a contest for kids of all ages who work in teams to design "technology of the future" for one-time awards of up to $10,000. **Navy ROTC** offers renewable full tuition and books at approximately 150 participating universities in exchange for a commitment to serve after graduation.

Sunday, January 27

Monday, January 28

Tuesday, January 29

☐ Tobisha/NSTA ExploraVision Awards. www.exploravision.org
☐ March SAT registration deadline

Wednesday, January 30

_____

_____

_____

Thursday, January 31

☐ Miami University (OH), application deadline
☐ Discover Card Tribute Award.
www.discoverfinancial.com
☐ Navy ROTC scholarship deadline.
www.todaysmilitary.com.

CONGRATULATIONS! YOU'RE A LUCKY WINNER!

Most people have seen the banner ads on the Internet that say, "If flashing, you're a winner!" Funny how those banners are always flashing.

The same thing happens in college admission. College applicants and their parents are particularly vulnerable to the congratulations-you've-won-something ploy. Take Who's Who among American High School Students, an official-sounding outfit that has been "honoring" students since 1967. Exactly how students are chosen for this great honor is not entirely clear. One way or

I urge students to choose one or two extracurriculars where they can make a real contribution rather than doing lots of insignificant ones.

—Counselor's heads-up

another, Who's Who gets names and addresses from educational and civic organizations. One high school counselor tells us that she herself got a Who's Who nomination, apparently as a result of doing a scholarship search on www.fastweb.com.

The game at Who's Who is simple: In exchange for seeing your son or daughter's name in tiny type, they hope you'll buy a copy of their weighty, hardcover tome. What is a listing in Who's Who worth on a college application? Not much more than a sigh and a roll of the eyes.

We had to insist that our son visit a couple of schools he hadn't considered. One of them ended up being one of his two final choices.

—University of San Diego mom

THE STANDARDIZED TESTING MONEY MACHINE

The College Board owns the SAT. Educational Testing Service (ETS) produces and administers it. Together, they take in hundreds of millions of dollars every year on the test. Watch your wallet. The standard fee for the SAT is $43, but miss a registration deadline and the price jumps to $65 for late registration and $80 to take it as a standby. Want to send scores to the colleges? College Board and ETS let you have four freebies at the time of registration, but if students want to see their scores before they send them, or they're not sure where they want to send the scores at the time they test, additional reports cost $9.50 per college. In a hurry? That's not good—the usual additional score-report procedure can take up to a month. But for only $26.50 extra (plus $9.50 per report), students can have their scores rushed in just two business days.

ACT operates from basically the same playbook, but with one major difference. Reporting all SAT and Subject Test results is cumulative—when you send a score, all your previous SAT and Subject Test scores are also sent. But with ACT, students can choose to send the scores from a particular date without sending the others. That idea is appealing to students and parents, but the downside is that students must pay for even more score reports.

Some high schools have helped families save a few bucks by putting test scores on the back of student transcripts. While many colleges have always held out for the "official" scores, others have taken scores from transcripts in lieu of receiving them directly from the test-makers. But this little racket may be on its last legs. Both the SAT and ACT now have an essay, and as each will be scanned into a computer, colleges can electronically access what students write. However, colleges have online access to those student essays only when students send their scores to the colleges through the College Board. (See page 42 for more on the new SAT.)

To avoid unnecessary fees that can run into hundreds of dollars, stay on top of registration and score-reporting deadlines.

This book lists dozens of scholarships and contests, most of which have fixed deadlines. The contests below have deadlines that vary by region, or have deadlines for local competitions that are a prelude to regional and national competitions. All are among the most prestigious competitions of their kind in the nation, and all can be entered by high schoolers of any age. Those who win in twelfth grade typically enter in the lower grades to hone their skills.

Scholastic Art and Writing Awards (grades 7–12). With 250,000 entries and 900 awards, SAWA is one of the largest student contests in the nation. Winners in twelfth grade are eligible for scholarships. Most deadlines are in January but vary by region of residence (www.scholastic.com/artandwritingawards).

National History Day (6–12). State contests are typically held in March, and winners advance to National History Day in June. Nine one-time scholarships of up to $1,000 are awarded (www.nationalhistoryday.org).

American Legion's National High School Oratorical Contest (9–12). Deadlines vary by state but are usually in winter. Offers one-time scholarships of up to $18,000 (www.legion.org).

Intel Science and Engineering Fair (9–12). An umbrella organization for five hundred regional science fairs generally held in March. Winners compete in the national fair in May for one-time scholarships of up to $50,000. Nearly five hundred fairs worldwide (www.sciserv.org/isef).

Junior Science and Humanities Symposium (9–12). Regional symposia in early spring showcase original research projects in math, science, and engineering. National symposium in May. Forty-eight one-time scholarships of up to $20,000 (www.jshs.org).

United States Senate Youth Program (11–12). Two winners per state get a week in Washington, D.C., and a one-time $5,000 scholarship. To be eligible, students must serve in elected office and be nominated by a school official or state-level administrator. Deadlines vary by state (www.hearstfdn.org/ussyp).

FEBRUARY 2008

WITH COLLEGE APPLICATIONS FINALLY out the door, the February blahs should be no big deal for the Class of 2008. Students are advised to log onto colleges' websites to make sure their applications are complete. Most financial aid deadlines arrive this month. Financial aid filers should watch for correspondence through the mail (paper filers) or online (electronic filers). Verify that your information is correct. Families with special financial circumstances should contact the colleges directly. (See page 187.)

Members of the Class of 2009 should continue researching colleges and meet with their college counselors if possible. Families should solidify plans for college visits during spring break and continue weighing summer options.

WHAT TO DO:

✓ **Friday, February 1**
Application deadlines at moderately selective colleges
Financial aid deadlines at highly selective colleges

✓ **Saturday, February 9**
ACT administered

✓ **Friday, February 15**
Application deadlines at moderately selective colleges

FEBRUARY 1–2, 2008

A slew of colleges have February 1 application deadlines, including **Dickinson, Franklin and Marshall, Lewis and Clark, University of San Francisco, University of Texas at Austin, University of Wisconsin at Madison,** and **Wofford**. February 1 is also D-Day for financial aid applications at highly selective institutions. (For a complete list of February 1 deadlines, see Appendix B.)

Junior Achievement, an organization that promotes business and economic literacy in schools, awards a range of scholarships with February 1 deadlines. **DAR** (Daughters of the American Revolution) also offers a range of scholarships related to U.S. history, government, economics, historic preservation, and health professions. (Various deadlines begin February 1.) The **National Peace Essay Contest** is one of the best known of its kind, with more than fifty one-time scholarships of up to $10,000. The **Phi Delta Kappa Scholarship** offers one-time scholarships of up to $5,000 to prospective education majors.

Although most college summer programs are simply vehicles for getting paying customers through the door, MIT's is a conspicuous exception. The **Minority Introduction to Engineering, Entrepreneurship, and Science** annually attracts many of the nation's ablest minority students and disadvantaged nonminorities. The **Women's Technology Program** is a magnet for the nation's top female students. It costs $2,000 for four weeks, but unlike many summer programs, the WTP provides generous need-based financial aid. Both programs are open to students in the summer after eleventh grade. (See Summer for Free, page 92.)

Friday, February 1

- ☐ Application deadlines at moderately selective colleges
- ☐ Announcement of National Merit Finalists
- ☐ Financial aid deadlines at highly selective private colleges
- ☐ Junior Achievement Scholarships. www.ja.org
- ☐ DAR Scholarships. www.dar.org

- ☐ National Peace Essay Contest. www.usip.org/ed/npec/index.html
- ☐ Phi Delta Kappa International Scholarship. www.pdkintl.org
- ☐ Women's Technology Program Deadline. wtp.mit.edu

_____

Saturday, February 2

- ☐ MIT Minority Introduction to Engineering, Entrepreneurship, and Science Summer Program. web.mit.edu/mites/www

_____

_____

_____

_____

FEBRUARY 3–9, 2008

February is one of the toughest times of the school year for everyone. The weather is still bad, half the students are generally sick, and spring break is still nowhere in sight. Fortunately, the week is a light one for deadlines. The **American Foreign Service Association** offers merit awards of up to $2,500 and need-based awards of up to $3,500, as well as an award for the best essay in its competition. **Tisch School of the Arts at NYU** offers one of the nation's elite summer programs in the performing arts; offerings include acting, dramatic writing, musical theater, and film. **MIT's Research Science Institute** is a small, elite program that attracts some of the nation's top technically oriented students. (The program recently expanded to include an additional session at Caltech.) For the Class of 2009, this week's ACT is the first of three available before the end of the school year.

Sunday, February 3

Monday, February 4

Tuesday, February 5

☐ American Foreign Service Association Scholarship. www.afsa.org

Wednesday, February 6

Thursday, February 7

☐ March SAT late-registration deadline

Friday, February 8

☐ Tisch School of the Arts Summer Program application deadline. www.nyu.edu

☐ Research Science Institute Deadline. www.cee.org/rsi

Saturday, February 9

☐ ACT Administered

People in places like Connecticut, Massachusetts, and New Jersey are forever complaining that they get the shaft in college admission, and when it comes to the National Merit Program, they're right.

The PSAT, and in particular the one students take in eleventh grade, is the qualifying test for the National Merit Program. About 3 percent of the eleventh grade test-takers are designated as Commended Students and receive a certificate for their efforts. The top 1.25 percent of test-takers, more or less, are designated as National Merit Semifinalists.

But back to Connecticut, Massachusetts, and New Jersey. Since National Merit mandates a fixed number of winners in each state that is proportional to its population, these states have much higher qualifying scores than places like South Dakota or Wyoming. In Massachusetts, the qualifying Selection Index (SI) score for Semifinalists varies from year to year, but is usually about 221 (SI = verbal score + math score + writing skills score). In Wyoming, the qualifying score is about 201. (If the thought of moving to Wyoming suddenly sounds appealing, see Top Ten Signs that Mom and Dad Are Losing It, page 33.)

Once the Semifinalists are announced—in September of twelfth grade—they have about a month to write an essay and complete a short application, which is coupled with a counselor recommendation. Advancing to Finalist is a snap as long as your grades are in the A range. About 90 percent of Semifinalists become Finalists when the new crop is announced in early February. From here, the highest scorers are awarded one-time scholarships from National Merit of up to $2,500. Major corporations also make awards, usually to Finalists who are dependents of their employees or residents of areas where they operate. About two hundred four-year colleges offer scholarships to Finalists, including some institutions that make a cottage industry of enrolling Finalists with full-ride scholarships. (Don't count on anything but a yawn from Ivy-caliber schools, which are overrun with applications from National Merit honorees.)

In all, just over half of Finalists receive a scholarship. Whether or not Finalists get money may have less to do with merit than where they choose to go to college, where they live, and where their parents work.

The Truth about Test Prep

Remember what your Mom told you about stuff that sounds too good to be true? (Hint: It probably is.) Chalk up standardized test prep as one of those topics. To hear the test prep companies tell it, all you have to do is fork over a few hundred dollars (well, maybe $1,000) to get an eye-popping score increase on the SAT—guaranteed! To investigate those claims, we did a survey of more than 800 students at seventy schools who had taken the SAT. We found that those students who did not take a prep course actually scored higher than those who did. Hmm.

Are we suggesting that preparing for standardized tests is useless? Hardly. Hundreds of students told us in their surveys that the key to beating the SAT is taking timed practice tests—not listening to lectures about the SAT, not talking about it with a tutor, but practicing real questions under real conditions and then analyzing their results. Our recent book, *Fiske Nailing the New SAT*, goes over our survey and gives our best advice on how to prepare for the SAT. We recommend a similar approach for the ACT and the SAT Subject Tests.

Of course, there are some instances when paying for test prep may be the right choice. Likely candidates for a prep course include:

- Students who need adult direction
- Students who need the structure of a course to stay focused
- Students who are enthusiastic and will do the homework

Student enthusiasm is the most important indicator of these. If a student must be dragged kicking and screaming into the course, the odds of success are low. When there is a choice, go for one-on-one tutoring, even if it is only for a few sessions, rather than a one-size-fits-all course. The latter are often useless except for the practice tests. Pay no attention to score-increase guarantees. The fine print usually says that you won't get your money back, but you will be treated to a second helping of what didn't work the first time. The most important part of an SAT prep course is the instructor, not the brand name on the door. If you're convinced that paying for test prep is the right move, find a tutor you can connect with and give it your best shot.

FEBRUARY 10–16, 2008

Institutions with February 15 application deadlines include private colleges such as **Drew, Gettysburg, Rollins,** and **College of Wooster,** and public universities such as **University of Kentucky** and **The College of New Jersey.** (For a complete list, see Appendix B.) Any family that plans to file an application for financial aid—no matter what the institution—is advised to do so by February 15.

For a mere $500 registration fee, the **Girls' Leadership Workshop** offers nine days of programming at Val-Kill, the one-time rural getaway cottage of Eleanor Roosevelt, who is the inspiration for the program. **U.S.A. Funds** offers one-time scholarships of up to $1,500 to minority students with financial need. The **National Federation of Independent Business** makes more than 400 awards of $1,000 to teens with innovative business ideas.

Sunday, February 10

_____
_____
_____

Monday, February 11

☐ NFIB Young Entrepreneur Awards.
www.nfib.com

_____

Tuesday, February 12

_____
_____
_____

_____
_____
_____

Wednesday, February 13

☐ Florida State University, application deadline

_____

_____

_____

_____

_____

Thursday, February 14

_____

_____

_____

_____

_____

_____

Friday, February 15

☐ Application deadlines at moderately selective colleges

☐ Girls' Leadership Workshop at Val-Kill application deadline. www.ervk.org/glw

☐ Financial aid deadlines at moderately selective private colleges and public universities

☐ U.S.A. Funds Access to Education Scholarship. www.usafunds.org

Saturday, February 16

_____

_____

_____

_____

_____

_____

FEBRUARY 17–23, 2008

This week, financial aid filers are advised to make sure that their applications are on track. When you applied for aid, your family should have received via email a copy of the FAFSA student aid report (SAR) and a similar document from the CSS/PROFILE. If there are special circumstances surrounding the aid application—such as a blip in income or unusual expenses or debts—write a letter directly to the financial aid office of every college where you are applying.

The **All-USA High School Academic Team** provides twenty one-time awards of $2,500 to twenty students nominated by their schools.

Sunday, February 17

_____

_____

_____

Monday, February 18

_____

_____

_____

Tuesday, February 19

_____

_____

_____

Wednesday, February 20

☐ All-USA High School Academic Team. School nomination required. www.usatoday.com

_____

Thursday, February 21

Friday, February 22

Saturday, February 23

FEBRUARY 24–29, 2008

If this February seems longer than most, you're not dreaming. Chalk it up to leap year. There could be no better time for the **Optimist International Essay Contest**, open to students in grades 9–12, which features one-time scholarships of up to $6,000. The February 28 deadline is for the national contest; check with local Optimist Clubs for entry procedures. (The Optimists also sponsor an oratory contest with a maximum award of $1,500.)

Sunday, February 24

Monday, February 25

Tuesday, February 26

Wednesday, February 27

Thursday, February 28

☐ University of British Columbia and Warren Wilson College, admission deadline

☐ Optimist International Essay Contest. www.optimist.org

Friday, February 29

College Essays: Window on the Soul or Just Plain Wacky?

When it comes to college essay topics, one never knows what the admission office will dream up. A recent topic at the University of Chicago was (we kid you not) "How do you feel about Wednesday?" Go figure. For years, Penn has asked the following mind-bender: "You have just completed your 300-page autobiography. Please submit page 217."

No wonder students dread these essays. The fact that many topics are straightforward is small consolation to the thousands of students who will soon enter a struggle to the death with one or more of them.

So why bring this up now? These essay questions are typical of the kind of reflectiveness the college search demands but that does not come naturally to many students. Some college counselors ask students to respond to essay questions while still in eleventh grade, not only to work on the writing process, but also to encourage a habit of thinking that will serve them well throughout the college process. Here are a few distinctive questions that have been used in recent years:

Chances are good that you're going to have one or more roommates at some point in your college years. What sort of person would make a good match for you? Explain why.

—Princeton University

Pearl Buck once said, "You cannot make yourself feel something you do not feel, but you can make yourself do right in spite of your feelings." Tell us about an experience where you felt that you "did the right thing" in spite of your feelings.

—Randolph College

If I could change the world, I would . . .

—University of Tulsa

Tell us about an opinion that you have had to defend or an incident in your life which placed you in conflict with the beliefs of a majority of people and explain how this affected your value system.

—MIT

Fortunately, most colleges let students have a choice of which questions they want to answer, and many simply ask students to write about a topic that is meaningful to them. But grappling with questions like these is a good exercise, whether or not the particular colleges are on your list.

PLANNING A SPRING COLLEGE VISIT

For eleventh graders, February is an ideal time to think about the possibility of college visits during spring break. Such visits can be better than those in the summer because college spring break tends to be earlier than the break for high schools, and therefore college classes may be in session. Although the admission office will be preoccupied with last year's class—and perks such as a night in the dorms are generally available only for twelfth graders—the plusses outweigh the minuses.

A parent's first impulse may be to grab the phone and call the college. Good thought, but slow down. The student should make the call while mom and dad cool their heels. As we never tire of pointing out, the college admission process is all about the student taking control. Besides, a few colleges will even track whether it was the student or you who made the call. (Nothing personal, but they prefer to hear from students.)

Although students may tremble at the thought of calling an admission office, the procedure is easy: Dial the phone, say you're an eleventh grader looking at colleges, say the date you're coming, and then ask about the possibility of a) a tour, b) a group information session, c) an interview, and d) contact with someone in a department or program of interest. The person on the other end of the line will have heard these requests a thousand times (and will likely be an administrative assistant who will not be involved in evaluating your application). A tour is the only sure thing, but students should find out how much of the rest is available. Small colleges are more likely to offer the personal touch than big universities, which usually don't offer campus interviews.

A spring-break visit is often a student's first real engagement with the college search. Parents can help by encouraging their son or daughter to take the lead.

Top Ten Signs that Mom and Dad Are Losing It

Call it Pre-College Stress Syndrome: the debilitating illness that causes Mom and Dad to take leave of their senses for months at a time. Parents may be suffering from PCSS if they:

10. Attend eleventh-grade college night while son is still in middle school.

9. Propose *Fiske Guide to Colleges* as their book club's selection of the month.

8. Put the high school college counselor's home phone number on speed dial.

7. Dig out old report cards to calculate daughter's GPA to .0001 accuracy.

6. Revive friendship with obnoxious in-law who graduated from Duke.

5. Send flowers to phone receptionists at Amherst, Wesleyan, and Carleton.

4. House-hunt in Wyoming to enhance child's "geo" appeal at the Ivies.

3. Tell friends that "we" are applying to Stanford and Berkeley.

2. Wake up daughter each morning with CD of Ivy League fight songs.

1. Put vanity license plates reading "730CR/770M" on the family SUV.

If any these sound familiar, have Mom and Dad reread the Parent's College Admission Pledge on page xxi.

MARCH 2008

WAITING REALLY IS THE HARDEST PART—just ask any college applicant. A few stray decision letters will arrive by early March, but most will not come until the last two weeks of the month. Families should scrutinize aid packages and make plans for a last round of college visits in April. Applicants to public institutions should keep a close eye on the procedures for getting a dorm room.

Juniors should use spring break for college visits and/or to prepare for standardized tests. Students in AP courses should make sure they are registered to take the exams.

WHAT TO DO:

✓ **Saturday, March 1**
Application and financial aid deadlines at moderately selective colleges
SAT administered

✓ **Friday, March 7**
April ACT registration deadline

✓ **Saturday, March 15**
Application deadlines at moderately selective colleges

MARCH 1, 2008

March 1 brings another spate of admission deadlines at moderately selective institutions, including **Austin College, Mills College, Ohio Wesleyan University, Rose-Hulman Institute,** and **Susquehanna University.** (For a complete list of March 1 deadlines, see Appendix B.) For the Class of 2009, the April ACT date is the preferred spring alternative at many high schools, though some students decide to wait until June when school is out in much of the country.

Kaplan's "My Turn" Essay Contest gives entrants in grades 9–12 a shot at seeing their work in *Newsweek*'s feature by the same name along with a one-time award of up to $5,000. The **Pfizer Epilepsy Scholarship Award**, offering one-time stipends of $3,000, is among the most prominent awards available to students with a particular medical condition.

The **Department of Agriculture 1890 Scholarship** offers full-ride renewable awards to students looking at historically black colleges. Clark's **Summer Science Program** is three weeks and free for the taking for students who have completed eleventh grade. **Carleton College** offers one of the nation's premier summer programs for minority students, the **Liberal Arts Experience**. The program is open to students between tenth and eleventh grade. The program is one week long and the college pays all expenses, including travel. (See Summer for Free, page 92.) CMU's **Summer Programs for Diversity** are free, six-week programs for rising eleventh and twelfth graders in math, science, and fine arts.

Saturday, March 1

- ☐ SAT administered
- ☐ Admission and financial aid deadlines at moderately selective institutions
- ☐ Kaplan/*Newsweek* "My Turn" Essay Contest. www.kaptest.com/essay
- ☐ Pfizer Epilepsy Scholarship Award. www.epilepsy-scholarship.com

- ☐ USDA 1890 National Scholars Program. 1890scholars.program.usda.gov
- ☐ Carnegie Mellon University—Summer Programs for Diversity. www.cmu.edu
- ☐ Carleton Liberal Arts Experience Summer Program. www.carleton.edu
- ☐ Clark University—Summer Science Program Deadline. www.clarku.edu

FOR PARENTS: SINGIN' THOSE PROCRASTINATION BLUES

There is no better symbol for the agonies of the college search than the tormented mother, unable to get her wayward son to think about where to go or what to study. (Daughters are also capable of procrastination, but sons are the undisputed champs.)

Why do these otherwise fine young men give their mothers such grief? Malice? Perverse sense of humor? Repressed conflicts from the oral phase? The dance done by mothers and sons is an elaborate one. Mom makes a suggestion. Son does the opposite. Mom decides to do herself what she has asked son to do. Son undermines what mom has done. And so it goes for a thoroughly unpleasant sixteen months until graduation.

Fear is the real reason for college-search procrastination, male or female. For a teen who has never experienced life away from home and has never been subjected to a comprehensive evaluation, the college search is a uniquely terrifying prospect. Few young people have developed the tools they need to deal with it. They are forced to do so as the process moves forward, but in the meantime their first response is to dig in their heels and deny. Seeing this, a parent's natural reaction is to push harder, much to the irritation of the student, who pushes back. Once set in motion, the pattern is hard to break. Here are some suggestions to help parents cope:

- **Bite your tongue.** Parents are always a step ahead of their kids on the college search. Don't fret when it doesn't move on your timetable. Make suggestions, ask questions, and drop reminders, but be prepared for a hasty retreat if you encounter resistance. Many eleventh graders have a hard time getting into the process. Everything will eventually work out.

- **Let others deliver the message.** Parents may not realize it, but they get dumber every year as their kids get older. By a kid's sixteenth birthday, parents are ignorant of any remotely useful information. Make an appointment with the school counselor and talk to him or her about the messages that you think should be conveyed. Then sit back and let someone else be the messenger.

• **Get them on a campus.** There is nothing like visiting a campus to make the process real. Students often find new motivation when they see all the incredible resources that will be at their disposal. If they sit in on an admission presentation, they suddenly realize the competition they'll be up against. For a first visit, almost any plausible college will do. Each visit to a college campus provides a basis for comparison on future visits.

Procrastination is the toughest nut for parents to crack. For advice on advanced cases, see page 121.

> My most productive college visits were the ones without my parents, where I actually stayed in a student's dorm or apartment, went out with them and their friends at night, and had them show me around the campus.
>
> —University of Southern California student

Early March is when many high schools begin course sign-ups for the following year. Students always face dilemmas. Do I bail out of Spanish V in order to take a third AP course? Should I continue with art or take a computer course? Do I really need to take calculus? And the bottom line: What will look good to the colleges?

> I see too many students spend four years establishing a fabulous GPA and activities résumé, then spend too little time on their applications.
>
> —Counselor's heads-up

The answer to the last one is simple. Highly selective colleges want to see top grades in the school's most challenging courses. Just because a student is interested in history doesn't mean colleges will give a free pass on math and science. A key element of every student's application is the high school counselor's rating of his or her curriculum. Most demanding available? Very demanding? Average? At Ivy-type schools, any rating that is not "most demanding" means that you had better be a star athlete or French horn prodigy.

There are always legitimate choices to make. For a student passionate about the life sciences, dropping Spanish V to pick up AP Environmental Science makes perfect sense. In electives like art and computer, a student's interests trump any thought of what might "look good."

In recent years, there has been a backlash against the mindless race to pile on AP courses. A few elite private schools have dumped the AP curriculum in favor of homegrown electives that cater to the interests of students and faculty. Colleges such as University of Chicago have gone on record saying they prefer students who have made intelligent choices in their course selection rather than simply accumulating every conceivable advanced course. (For more on the AP program, see page 78.)

In today's climate of hyperanxiety, parents must help their kids make sane choices. Mental health is important, too. Happy and productive students are the ones most likely to excel in all phases of twelfth grade—including the college admission game.

MARCH 2–8, 2008

A peek into next week shows that March 15 is the deadline for students to register to take AP exams in May. If you are currently enrolled in an AP course, your school will probably register you automatically to take the exam. The fee is about $84 with limited financial assistance available that may vary from school to school. Check with the school's AP coordinator. About 60 percent of schools nationwide offer AP courses. If you want to take an AP exam but attend one of the 40 percent of schools that do not offer AP, or if you are homeschooled, now is the time to contact a school in your area that does offer them. Students considering this option should head to www.collegeboard.com for an overview of the tests or buy a prep book among the many that are available in bookstores. AP courses are generally a year long, so covering all the material will take some doing.

All-around academic and athletic excellence is the standard for the **Scholar Athlete Milk Mustache of the Year** award, which echoes the popular advertising campaign with the same theme. Twenty-five one-time scholarships of $7,500 are awarded.

Sunday, March 2

_____   _____

_____   _____

Monday, March 3

_____   _____

_____   _____

Tuesday, March 4

_____   _____

_____   _____

Wednesday, March 5

☐ Scholar Athlete Milk Mustache of the Year   _____
   (SAMMY) Award. www.bodybymilk.com
                                                      _____

Thursday, March 6

_____   _____

_____   _____

Friday, March 7

☐ April ACT registration deadline   _____

_____   _____

Saturday, March 8

_____   _____

_____   _____

THE SAT GETS A MAKEOVER

Good-bye, 1600. With the advent of the new SAT in 2005, the supreme symbol of standardized testing brainpower became 2400.

So long, SAT Verbal. Students now do battle with two new sections: critical reading and writing. Mere oval-blackening is out, replaced by a twenty-five-minute essay.

These are the most notable features of the new SAT. Despite the essay requirement and the College Board's lengthening the test by forty-five minutes (to three hours and forty-five minutes), the changes were not all bad. The much-feared analogy section has been scrapped, and so has the bane of the math section: quantitative comparisons.

Although the SAT has undergone nearly a dozen overhauls in its seventy-seven-year history, this one may be the most significant. The College Board always claimed that the test measures all-around reasoning ability rather than achievement in particular courses. But a growing chorus of critics accused the test of being too disconnected from what students learn in school. The analogy section was a particularly notable example: When was the last time an English class sat down to ponder those mind-benders?

According to the Board, the current SAT is a better reflection of what should be learned in a typical high school curriculum. Here is a breakdown of what to expect:

- **Critical Reading.** This is the name for the old Verbal section. The familiar reading comprehension passages of approximately 400–850 words are still there. To replace the analogies, the College Board added a batch of shorter reading passages of about 100–200 words.

- **Writing.** This new section includes questions similar to those on the old SAT II Writing Test. The multiple-choice questions

> Don't visit more than two colleges in a day. You get bored and tired and college number three won't get a fair chance.
>
> —University of Delaware student

ask students to identify grammar and usage errors and improve the wording of sentences and paragraphs. The essay asks students to state an opinion on a general topic and back it up with evidence taken from their reading and experiences.

• **Math.** The old SAT stopped with algebra and geometry. The current version includes topics often covered in Algebra II, from absolute value to quadratic functions. The test also features more challenging geometry, including questions where trigonometry can be used as an alternative method to find the answer. A touch of probability and statistics is also included.

Everyone who is stressed about new SAT can console themselves with the knowledge that some of the mystery surrounding the test has been dispelled. The College Board no longer claims that it is a yardstick of intelligence, reasoning ability, or anything similar. Rather, the test is now intended to measure past and future performance in school. We can all hope that a more straightforward and reliable SAT will be the ultimate result. Students taking the test in March should consider doing so a second time in May, with June devoted to the SAT Subject Tests.

> At larger schools, I felt like a walking version of my SAT score.
>
> —Southwestern University student

MARCH 9–15, 2008

The week's admission deadlines include **University of Minnesota at Morris** and **Wittenberg University**. With spring break around the corner, now is the time to follow through on making arrangements for college visits.

The **Horace Mann Scholarship** offers twenty-six one-time scholarships of up to $10,000 for children of teachers and other school employees. Among the nation's most unique summer programs is the **Freeman Asian Cultural Experience** in Sewanee, which offers a free two-week program for students who have completed tenth or eleventh grade. (See Summer for Free, page 92.) Looking ahead to summer, **Landmark Volunteers** offers dozens of community service programs throughout the nation. The program is available to students who have completed grades 9–11 and costs $1,250 in the form of a tax-deductible contribution. Students who apply after March 15 pay a higher fee. The **Hispanic Scholarship Fund** and the **Society of Hispanic Professional Engineers** team up to offer one-time awards of up to $2,500 for students with intended majors in math, computer science, and engineering.

Sunday, March 9

_____

_____

Monday, March 10

_____

_____

Tuesday, March 11

_____

_____

Wednesday, March 12

_____   _____

_____   _____

Thursday, March 13

_____   _____

_____   _____

Friday, March 14

_____   _____

_____   _____

Saturday, March 15

☐ Application deadlines at moderately selective colleges

☐ AP Exam registration deadline for homeschooled students and those attending schools not offering AP

☐ Horace Mann Scholarship. www.horacemann.com

☐ Landmark Volunteers Deposit Deadline. www.volunteers.com

☐ FACES Asian Studies Summer Program Deadline. www.sewanee.edu

☐ Hispanic Scholarship Funds deadline. www.hispanicfund.org

☐ Hispanic Scholarship Fund/Society of Hispanic Professional Engineers Scholarship Program. www.shpe.org

MARCH 16–22, 2008

With a late-March lull in the calendar, it makes sense for the Class of 2009 to look toward the crucial standardized tests of April, May, and June. Many students who took the March SAT will want a second shot at the test in May. Others may choose to wait until June—especially if they will have extra time to prepare because school is out—but June is also the traditional time for juniors to take the SAT Subject Tests.

Highly selective private colleges, and a few public institutions such as the **University of California**, require the Subject Tests. Before the advent of the new SAT and its writing section, such colleges almost universally required three Subject Tests, but now that the SAT includes Writing, most colleges have reduced their requirement to two tests. A representative sample of these includes **Amherst, Brown, Boston University, Connecticut College, Middlebury, NYU, Pomona, Rice**, and the **UC system.** The handful of hold-outs that still require three include **Harvard, Princeton, Yale, MIT**, and **Georgetown.** Students may take up to three Subject Tests on a single test date and cannot take them on the same date as an SAT. June is generally the recommended date because many students will have just finished a year of studying the subjects. For a complete list of all the schools that require Subject Tests, see Appendix A.

A few of the hundreds of colleges that do not require or recommend SAT Subject Tests are **Colby, University of Denver, George Washington, Gettysburg, Kalamazoo, Marquette**, and **Rhodes.** For most students looking at moderately selective schools, there is no reason to worry about the Subject Tests. However, homeschooled applicants and those from so-so high schools may want to consider the Subject Tests, even when their colleges do not require them, as a way to enhance their credentials. The **Ayn Rand Institute** offers awards of up to $2000 to ninth and tenth-graders for essays on Rand's novel *Anthem*.

Sunday, March 16

_____

_____

_____

Monday, March 17

_____

_____

_____

Tuesday, March 18

☐ Ayn Rand Essay Contest.
www.aynrand.org/contests

Wednesday, March 19

Thursday, March 20

Friday, March 21

☐ April ACT late-registration deadline

Saturday, March 22

MARCH 23–31, 2008

The waiting for the class of 2008 is almost over—many decision letters from selective colleges will come this week. The **Young American Creative Patriotic Art** award features three one-time scholarships of $10,000 and is available to students in grades 9–12. One of the nation's biggest providers of scholarships for minority students, the **Jackie Robinson Foundation,** offers scholarships of up to $25,000 over four years for students with outstanding credentials who are American citizens.

Sunday, March 23

Monday, March 24

Tuesday, March 25

Wednesday, March 26

Thursday, March 27

Friday, March 28

_____

_____

Sunday, March 30

_____

_____

Saturday, March 29

_____

_____

Monday, March 31

☐ Young American Creative Patriotic Art Award.
www.ladiesauxvfw.org

☐ Jackie Robinson Foundation Scholarship.
www.jackierobinson.org

SAT AND ACT: WHAT'S THE DIFFERENCE?

Ask someone from Massachusetts about the ACT and you may get a blank stare. The same goes if you ask about the SAT in Iowa. The world of college admission is divided into two fiefdoms of

> The most common mistake students make on the essay is to write as if they were doing an English paper—they do not allow their voices to be heard.   —Counselor's heads-up

roughly the same size. The SAT was created by a group of Ivy Leaguers and has historically been a sorting mechanism for elite East Coast institutions and their followers. The SAT is also the dominant test on the West Coast. The ACT came out of the University of Iowa and has historically served the Midwest and Mountain West.

The ACT includes sections scored from 1–36 in English, math, reading, and science reasoning.

Like the SAT, the ACT has added an essay section that is 30 minutes long. But unlike the SAT writing section, the ACT essay writing section is optional. (Consult your colleges to see if they require the essay.) The national average for the ACT is between 20 and 21, while the average on the SAT is about 500 on each of the writing, critical reading, and math sections.

The vast majority of colleges will accept either the SAT or ACT to satisfy their core testing requirements. Some highly selective institutions, especially technically oriented places, prefer the SAT because it makes finer distinctions on the high end of the testing range. Any student for whom standardized testing is a strong point should seriously consider taking the SAT.

Though used interchangeably, the tests differ in important ways. The SAT has historically emphasized vocabulary, reading comprehension, and logic. It makes heavy use of "distracters," especially in the math section, which are wrong answers made to look like correct ones. Confident, aggressive problem-solvers who know when people are trying to trick them will do best on the SAT. Relative to the SAT, the ACT is a more straightforward measure of achievement. Students who work hard in school—as opposed to those who are intuitive geniuses—tend to do well on it.

The changes to the SAT in 2005 narrowed the gap between the two tests. The multiple-choice questions on the SAT writing section resemble those in the ACT's English section, and the SAT's math section now includes advanced material that aligns it more closely with the ACT math. Although the current SAT is more like the ACT than the old one was, the tests do retain their distinct personalities.

The tests are similar in two additional ways: Both put students under time pressure and both are grueling marathons.

> We set deadlines for completion of applications tied to other events, like you can't go skiing at Christmas unless the applications are done by Thanksgiving.
>
> —Skidmore College mom

Most college counselors have had the unpleasant task of sitting down with a B+ student who wants to apply to Harvard, Yale, and Princeton with Penn as the backup school. Since unrealistic expectations tend to run in families, Mom and Dad are often in on the delusion. Part of the problem is that selective colleges are vastly more competitive for admission than they were a generation ago. But the importance of a reality check is crucial, especially at the beginning before anyone's heart is set on a pie in the sky.

Sitting down with the college counselor is a good first step. Often, counselors keep records of how applicants from the school have fared in the past. If the last eight students who have applied to a particular school with your grades and test scores have been denied, that's a clue of what is coming. Counselors are in the business of being professional pessimists when it comes to highly selective schools, and with good reason. They've seen a lot of dreams get dashed. Some are guilty of lowballing a student's prospects on occasion, so don't get discouraged if you think the counselor is selling your chances short.

Another tool in assessing admission chances is the college's profile, which lists ranges for grades and test scores. If a college accepts a third of its applicants or less, a student must have credentials significantly above average (or a special talent) in order to have an even chance of getting in. If a college accepts more than half, students who match the academic profile are likely to get in.

Ambitious applicants should hedge their bets. Most applicants have no trouble identifying dream schools, which are often highly selective. It is also a good idea to include several colleges where the odds are close to 50/50, and then at least two where the odds of admission are likely. Most importantly, every school on the list should be a good match for the student's needs and interests.

> Avoid "ego-booster" applications. Our daughter told us that she wanted to apply to one of the top schools just to see if she could get in. We reminded her that if she was not serious about these places, there was no point in wasting the time and money.
>
> —University of Illinois at Urbana-Champaign dad

APRIL 2008

LET'S HOPE THAT APRIL will not be the cruelest month for the Class of 2008. Most highly selective institutions will post their decisions on the Internet by April 1 with letters following early in the week of April 3. Wait-listed students should follow up promptly and vigorously. Financial aid applicants who get lowball awards from their top-choice college may appeal—preferably using a second, higher award as leverage. (See page 210.) Students wishing to take a year off before college should contact the colleges by phone and follow up with a letter. Students should reply to all offers of admission—including those they choose not to accept—by May 1.

Eleventh graders should continue researching colleges with a goal of finding ten to twelve likely options by the end of school. Families should firm up summer plans and schedule college visits.

WHAT TO DO:

✓ **Tuesday, April 1**
Decisions at the most selective colleges mailed and available on the Web; May SAT and Subject Tests registration deadline

✓ **Saturday, April 12**
ACT administered

April 1–5, 2008

Twelfth graders can expect decision letters from the last of their colleges this week and will have until May 1 to respond. Less-selective institutions with application deadlines this week include the University of Oklahoma and the University of Utah.

As the Class of 2008 mulls its options, the Class of 2009 should gather a few lessons for next year. Eleventh graders can learn a lot by watching their older friends deal with the final stages of the college search. For instance, there is probably at least one student in the Class of 2008 who applied to, say, twelve colleges. That person was probably admitted at eight schools, more or less, and now has the impossible task of trying to choose one from an unwieldy list of colleges. Lesson: It does not make sense to apply to more than six or eight colleges.

There are other scenarios to watch for. Did anybody in the Class of 2008 aim too high and get turned down at every school except for an undesired safety? Did anybody come to grief because their parents decided at the last minute that they could not afford Dream U? Look for pitfalls to avoid, and get pointers from the students whose college search turned out right.

The **Yoshiyama Award**, based solely on community service, requires a nomination and nets winners a one-time award of $5,000. The **Young Naturalist Awards** program gives one-time prizes of up to $2,500 to students in grades 7–12 for outstanding science projects in biology, earth science, or astronomy. (YNA is sponsored by the American Museum of Natural History.)

Tuesday, April 1

- ☐ May SAT and Subject Tests, registration deadline
- ☐ Decisions at highly selective colleges mailed and available on the Web; application deadlines at moderately selective universities.

- ☐ Yoshiyama Award.
  www.hitachifoundation.org/yoshiyama
- ☐ Young Naturalist Awards.
  www.amnh.org

Wednesday, April 2

_____

_____

_____

Thursday, April 3

_____

_____

_____

Friday, April 4

_____

_____

_____

_____

_____

_____

Saturday, April 5

_____

_____

_____

_____

_____

_____

APRIL 6–12, 2008

Mid-April offers the newly admitted a chance for a triumphant victory tour. Most colleges host roll-out-the-red-carpet days for accepted students at about this time, and it makes sense to do one last visit if there is any uncertainty about where to go. Such programs allow students to see the campus once again—with the eight-hundred-pound monkey of admission off their backs—and students also get to rub shoulders with their future classmates. Considering the amount of money that you will be forking over for tuition, the expense of one more trip is a small price to pay.

Eleventh graders planning summer college visits should set their itinerary and call now for the best chance of getting an interview. (See page 86.)

Sunday, April 6

_____   _____

_____   _____

_____   _____

Monday, April 7

_____   _____

_____   _____

_____   _____

Tuesday, April 8

_____

_____

_____

Wednesday, April 9

_____

_____

Thursday, April 10

☐ May SAT and Subject Tests late-registration
   deadline

_____

_____

_____

Friday, April 11

_____

_____

_____

_____

_____

_____

Saturday, April 12

☐ ACT Administered

_____

_____

_____

_____

WHAT FLATTERY WILL GET YOU

The National Youth Leadership Forum is the most prominent organization on the college prep scene that did not exist twenty years ago. Today, thousands of students are plied with invitations to attend its programs to the tune of more than $1,000 per week plus transportation expenses. Are these programs worth it? Students and parents nationwide want to know.

NYLF is a powerhouse of marketing and an interesting study in persuasion. The organization runs dozens of five- and ten-day programs annually, in cities throughout the country, that focus on Medicine, Law, Technology, and Defense/Intelligence/Diplomacy. NYLF builds its mailing list in a variety of ways, but one of the most important is by currying favor with high school teachers. It aggressively seeks "nominations" from them, cagily asking that they provide the names and addresses of students with the admonition that "space in the program is strictly limited." Only students with a 3.3 GPA may be nominated—about half the student body at many schools.

Armed with its nominations, NYLF mails its pitch to the students—not as a money-grubbing solicitor, but to bestow recognition on students who are starved for positive feedback and résumé builders. In reality, NYLF on the résumé means about as much as Who's Who among American High School Students (in other words, not much). A small fraction of attendees receive financial aid, but every college admission office knows that wealthy families who can pay the bill are the primary constituency.

But what about the programs? From everything we can gather, they are very good. At a recent Forum on Medicine, students heard lectures from leading medical professionals, visited medical schools, and completed a diagnosis simulation like those done by medical students. A recent Forum on Technology allowed students to meet with executives from Dell and IBM, among others.

Students generally enjoy the NYLF experience—especially the opportunity to make new friends who share their interests. It is NYLF's methods of persuasion rather than its programs that make many educators and us uncomfortable. Attending an NYLF program is not a meaningful honor, but it may be worthwhile depending on the student's interests and the family budget.

ADMISSION 101: THE BIG PICTURE

Many students (and parents) never get beyond the idea that college admission is a cold calculation of grades and test scores. They picture faceless committees passing judgment with ruthless efficiency on the hapless souls with the audacity to send in an application.

> Way too many colleges say that they don't emphasize SAT or ACT scores in the admission process.
>
> —Counselor's heads-up

Grades and scores are important, just as experience and references are important in getting a job. No one can get into college—or get a job—if they're not qualified. But qualifications only take you so far. The clincher is often the human element—the ability to interact, to make oneself vulnerable, and to have a conversation with admission officers across the chasm of a process that, because of its scale, does risk being impersonal.

Picture a college admission officer. Did he or she get into this job to be a standardized test bean counter? A transcript analysis technician? Are admission officers in it for the money? Strange as it may seem, most admission people stay in their jobs because they like working with teenagers. They want and even crave contact with applicants. Though buffeted by administrative pressures, they cherish the notion that they can make a difference.

Students must never lose sight of the real people who orchestrate the process. Call, write, email, interview—anything to keep a real conversation going without obvious brown-nosing or attention-getting stunts. It isn't easy, but students with the moxie to put themselves on the line are generally rewarded.

> Make sure that your tour guide is realistic. There is no school that only has good characteristics. Search for the flaws.
>
> —College of Charleston student

How to Jump-Start the College Search

Building a manageable list of college options—say, ten to twelve colleges—is one of the most important tasks in the spring of eleventh grade. Here is a list of ways to do it.

- **Read the One-Hour College Finder in the** *Fiske Guide to Getting into the Right College*. You'll find thumbnail sketches, organized by category, of several hundred of the nation's top colleges. For comprehensive descriptions, consult the *Fiske Guide to Colleges*.

- **Run an Internet search.** The Web is great for generating lists of colleges with particular criteria. You can sort by size, location, major, and dozens more traits. Our choice among the many sites is www.collegeboard.com.

- **Poll friends, teachers, and relatives.** Suggest that your son or daughter talk to students in grade twelve who share their interests. Contact friends currently in college when they come home for summer vacation.

- **Talk to some experts.** We've said it before—if you have a career interest, try to find a contact in the field. When planning a college visit, make an appointment with someone in a department or field you are considering. Most faculty will give you honest advice even if it doesn't steer you to their school.

- **Read college catalogues and viewbooks.** Most of this material falls under the heading of glitzy advertising, so look for the substance rather than the sizzle, such as course offerings, majors, and distribution requirements.

- **Talk to your counselor.** At schools with strong college counseling, this approach may be best of all. School counselors have the advantage of knowing you and knowing the colleges. Nine times out of ten, their advice is worth heeding.

THE COLLEGE SEARCH IN CYBERSPACE

Today's generation of students would rather log on than grab a pen and paper. It is now possible to point and click your way to college—at least most of the way. Here are some ways that the Internet comes in handy:

- **Electronic test registration.** The College Board (www.collegeboard.com) and ACT (www.act.org) are going all out to encourage families to register for the SAT and ACT online. Confirmation of registration is immediate and there is an email reminder before the test day for anyone with very early Alzheimer's.

- **Searching for colleges.** Websites ranging from the College Board to Princeton Review (www.princetonreview. com) and *U.S. News & World Report* (www.usnews.com) have search features that allow students to make choices in dozens of categories such as size, location, intended major, selectivity, and student life. With just a few clicks, students can generate a list of schools that share the qualities they seek.

- **Financial aid estimation and scholarships.** Head to www.collegeboard.com or www.finaid.org and click on "financial aid estimation." Within fifteen minutes, families can get an estimate of how much they will be expected to pay for college. For the Web's best free scholarship search site, head to www.fastweb.com.

- **College websites.** You'll find virtually everything at the college's website that you would find in its publications—and then some. A hint: Instead of going directly to the college's official website, do a category search in Yahoo! or your favorite search engine. You'll learn loads of interesting tidbits from student-produced sites, such as the online version of the campus newspaper.

Filing applications online is another popular use of the Web. (See page 136.) One thing you can't find on the Web is a place for candid, authoritative evaluations of the nation's best colleges. For that, you'll need to find a copy of another volume in the Fiske series, the *Fiske Guide to Colleges*.

APRIL 2008

April 13–19, 2008

By now, most students in the Class of 2008 will have figured out where they are going next fall. If that includes you, don't procrastinate about sending in your acceptance of the offer with a deposit (and sending a brief Dear John letter to the other schools). Colleges often settle important details like housing on a first-come, first-served basis. If you are given a choice of dorms and don't have a clue, contact a current student who graduated from your high school, or simply call the admission office and ask to speak to one. All dorms are not created equal.

The **Signet Classic Essay contest** offers five scholarships of $1,000 to eleventh and twelfth graders who write a two- to three-page essay. The **AMVETS Scholarship** offers ten awards totaling $4,000 each to veterans and their dependents.

Sunday, April 13

Monday, April 14

Tuesday, April 15

☐ Signet Classic Essay Contest.
www.penguingroup.com.

☐ AMVETS Scholarship deadline.
www.amvets.org

Wednesday, April 16

Thursday, April 17

Friday, April 18

Saturday, April 19

April 20–26, 2008

For the Class of 2008, a few last-minute scholarship opportunities remain. The **Ayn Rand Essay Contest**, sponsored by the foundation that carries on the work of the famed novelist and philosopher, offers sixteen one-time awards between $1,000 and $10,000 for essays on *The Fountainhead*. The contest is open to eleventh and twelfth graders. The **Society of Hispanic Engineers** offers scholarships of up to $3,000 via a variety of programs.

Sunday, April 20

☐ Society of Hispanic Engineers Scholarship deadline. www.shpe.org

_____

Monday, April 21

_____

_____

_____

Tuesday, April 22

_____

_____

_____

_____

_____

Wednesday, April 23

_____

_____

_____

Thursday, April 24

_____

_____

_____

Friday, April 25

☐ Ayn Rand Essay Contest. www.aynrand.org/contests

_____

_____

Saturday, April 26

_____

_____

_____

APRIL
2008

APRIL 27–30, 2008

A glance into next week reveals that May 6 is the deadline for eleventh graders to register for the June SAT. For those in the Class of 2009 aiming at highly selective colleges, most counselors recommend this date for the SAT Subject Tests. Those looking at schools that don't require the Subject Tests may want to think about taking another SAT, or consider taking the ACT on June 14 (deadline May 9). Our recommendation to consider the ACT is particularly strong for those who were disappointed with their SAT scores and may do better on the ACT.

The **Holocaust Remembrance Project Essay Contest,** open to students in grades 9–12, makes ten one-time awards of up to $10,000, along with smaller cash prizes.

Sunday, April 27

_____

_____

_____

Monday, April 28

_____

_____

_____

Sunday, April 29

_____

_____

_____

Monday, April 30

☐ Holocaust Remembrance Project Essay Contest. www.holocaust.hklaw.com

_____

WHEN MOM AND DAD RUN AMOK: COLLEGE COUNSELORS TELL ALL

You know they mean well, but sometimes parents do the dumbest things. High school counselors see more than their share of these bloopers and mis-steps. We asked the Fiske College Counselors Advisory Group, listed on page 249, to discuss the most common parental mistakes. Here are a few excerpts:

- "I had a parent who called the admission office of a particular college on a weekly basis. In the end, the admission rep called me to say that they were not taking the student because the father had been such a pest. He had even told them that he was retiring at the end of the school year and that the family planned to move near the college and he wanted to volunteer in the admission office!"

- "In my opinion, one of the biggest mis-takes parents make is looking only at 'name brand' schools as possibilities for their children. There are so many fantastic colleges out there, yet many,

if not most, go virtually unnoticed because parents and students alike get stuck on the rankings they read about in major magazines such as *U.S. News*."

- "Parents make the mistake of opening the student's mail. This is a big no-no. Students are not accustomed to getting mail, and then suddenly in tenth and eleventh grade, they feel important! One of my parents was so eager to read the outcome for her son's college appli-cation that she proceeded to steam it open over the teakettle. She never expected that the letter would actually catch on fire! So she had to put the burnt letter on the table with a Post-it note—confessing this act to her son."

> **Start early because students have so much to deal with their senior year that they are sometimes overwhelmed.**
>
> **—University of San Diego mom**

- "Families need to understand the role of the counselor. They make the mistake of thinking that the counselor's job is to get their child into their top-choice colleges, no matter how unreasonable that choice may be. They seem to think that we can persuade Harvard to take a B student because we have a buddy-buddy relationship with Bill Fitzsimmons. Sometimes our relationships can work with borderline students, but colleges want students who will succeed at their schools."

> Very few parents understand how the admission process has changed in the last decade. Colleges that they think are backups simply aren't.
>
> —Counselor's heads-up

- "The one piece of advice I give most regularly is to back off. When a parent pushes too early, or expresses a strong preference for one of the colleges a student is choosing between, the student usually balks and the result is the opposite of what the parent intended. Our charges are at the brink of adulthood and make their own choices. They are programmed to struggle for their independence, and wise parents respect that and guide them only with the lightest of touches."

- "I had a senior who was accepted to her first-love school—Georgetown. She was also accepted to Texas A&M with a full-ride scholarship. Her parents took her to Georgetown several times for visits and programs and encouraged her and were excited with her through the entire application process. In April, they decided they did not want her to go that far from home and insisted she accept A&M's offer. She was devastated but did what her parents asked. After seeing their daughter's spirit and enthusiasm leave her, they relented (on May 2) and said she could go to Georgetown. I think realizing that their daughter would actually give up her dream to please them opened their eyes to what they were doing."

A PITCH FOR SMALL COLLEGES

Their names don't necessarily set hearts aflutter. Places like College of Wooster, Whitman, or Guilford—to name three—are beneath the radar screen of the cocktail-party circuit. They're among the dozens of small liberal arts colleges enrolling roughly one thousand to three thousand students that dot the national landscape. Small colleges are out of favor in today's college admission game. Everybody wants to go where the action is—to do the internship scene in Washington, join the cast of thousands in Berkeley, or rub shoulders with the bohemians in Greenwich Village. With some exceptions, small colleges tend to be in out-of-the-way places, and a disproportionate number of good ones are in the Midwest, far from the nation's glamor spots.

We don't deny that large institutions in exciting cities are the right choice for many students. We simply think it is unfortunate that so many students won't even consider small colleges. A few of their advantages include:

- **Quality teaching.** Small colleges nearly always provide more access to faculty than big ones. And with only undergraduates on campus, students have a better shot at research opportunities.

- **A well-rounded life.** Any student who loves being involved in many different activities should consider a small college, where the student government, the newspaper, and other organizations are more accessible to the typical student.

- **A place to belong.** Studies consistently show that students do better academically when they are involved in the life of their community. Being a face in the crowd often appeals to students who have overdosed on high school, but, in the end, the reality of anonymity may not be so wonderful.

The issue of large versus small is an important one for many students, and there are additional plusses and minuses on both sides. A more thorough weighing of this issue can be found in the *Fiske Guide to Getting into the Right College.*

THE LONG AND WINDING ROAD TO AN ATHLETIC SCHOLARSHIP

From the time they were knee-high, many high school students have fantasized about playing sports in college and beyond. To make the dream a reality takes persistence, nerve, major athletic talent—and an early start on the college selection process. By spring of eleventh grade, aspiring athletes should be contacting coaches and expressing interest. But before we offer advice to athletic hopefuls, a discussion of the pitfalls of college sports are in order. Most importantly:

- **Playing in college is a huge commitment.** Even at the Division III level, the necessary effort dwarfs what it takes in high school. Long hours of practice and in-season road trips sap energy that would otherwise be available for schoolwork.

- **Getting a spot is harder than it used to be.** The days are over when better-than-average high school athletes could walk on. Today's generation of students is primed to compete for scholarships, or to get the admission advantage that comes from being a Division III recruited athlete.

- **Be prepared to apply early.** Many coaches pressure applicants to apply ED or EA. They say, in not so many words, that if you don't apply early, they can't help you. Be ready to file your application as early as September of twelfth grade, and think ahead about how you will react when a coach starts leaning on you. Don't be buffaloed into a commitment if better choices are out there.

- **Coaches can be sleazebags.** There—we said it. Many coaches have integrity, but others play a shell game. The drill: Recruit five students for one spot on the team, then dump the four also-rans when the real first choice signs on the dotted line.

> Don't apply to eighteen colleges like I did! Either narrow down your choices or start saving now for application fees.
>
> —**University of Texas at Austin student**

Some students assume that Division III schools are less concerned about athletics than those in Division I or II, but that is not always the case. Although they don't give scholarships, elite small colleges have the highest percentage of students who are recruited athletes. These colleges may not play on national TV, but colleges assume that a victory over Archrival U makes the old grads happy and can mean big bucks in donations.

The first step in becoming a recruited athlete is to talk to the high school or club coach. Students should ask for an honest evaluation and get suggestions for colleges where they might fit in. The next step is to crank out letters—lots of them—to express interest. Pertinent information may include club tournaments or summer camps where the student will be playing. A one-page sports résumé should generally go along with the letter, and with some sports, families should make a video showing skill drills or game highlights. If the high school or club coach volunteers to contact a college coach, so much the better.

A few athletes won't have to bother with any of this. They are the superstars all the coaches want. The vast majority of aspiring athletes might be good enough, could be good enough, and must hustle for everything they get.

> **Admission officers at highly selective colleges are too enthusiastic during interviews. Students leave those meetings encouraged to apply, even if they stand no chance of getting in.**
>
> —Counselor's heads-up

MAY–JUNE 2008

IF YOU'VE EVER WONDERED WHAT drinking from a fire hose is like, try taking three AP tests in a two-week span. Both juniors and seniors will have the pleasure of this experience beginning May 1. Waitlisted seniors should continue to follow up with these colleges. Families should watch for mailings from First Choice U, especially with regard to housing and course registration. Families should make plans to attend summer orientation programs where applicable.

After APs are over, the Class of 2009 should turn its attention to the SAT Subject Tests in June, and also consider taking the June ACT.

WHAT TO DO:

✓ **Saturday, May 3**
SAT and Subject Tests administered

✓ **May 5–16**
AP exams

✓ **Tuesday, May 6**
June SAT and Subject Tests, registration deadline

✓ **Friday, May 9**
June ACT registration deadline

✓ **Saturday, June 7**
SAT and Subject Tests administered

✓ **Saturday, June 14**
ACT administered

MAY 1–3, 2008

May 1 is the day of decision for the Class of 2008, and it is a deadline not to be trifled with. Applicants who procrastinate past this day without sending a deposit to their college of choice risk losing their place in the class. When more students accept a college's offer of admission than it expects, the threat is real. Families should also understand that sending deposits to two institutions is considered dirty pool. By doing so, they're keeping a hapless waitlisted student in limbo while they take their sweet time in deciding where to go.

Institutions with May 1 application deadlines include **Colorado School of Mines, University of Hawaii at Manoa,** and **Texas Tech**. The **Jane Austen Society** offers a prize of $1,000 for first place in its essay contest, open to students in grades 9–12. The June ACT, with its registration deadline next week, is the last standardized test administered before fall.

Thursday, May 1

- ☐ Candidate's reply date, Class of 2008
- ☐ Application deadlines at moderately selective colleges

- ☐ Jane Austen Society Essay Contest. www.jasna.org

Friday, May 2

Saturday, May 3

MAY 4–10, 2008

AP exam week is the final reckoning for students who have spent an entire year reading, writing, and cramming. In many schools, students can take the morning off from school prior to an afternoon AP, or the afternoon off for an exam the next morning. Scores usually arrive in the mail at school in early July, though students can call and get their scores by phone beginning July 1 for the incredibly low price of $8. The upside of surviving APs is that the final few weeks of school are usually a piece of cake.

The **American Fire Sprinkler Association Essay Contest** is a well-known if esoteric competition with ten one-time scholarships of up to $2,000.

Sunday, May 4

_____

_____

Monday, May 5

☐ AP U.S. Government and Politics Exam (morning)

☐ AP Comparative Government Exam, AP French Language Exam (afternoon)

Tuesday, May 6

☐ June SAT and Subject Tests, registration deadline

☐ AP Computer Science A Exam, AP Computer Science AB exam, AP Spanish Language Exam (morning)

☐ AP Statistics Exam (afternoon)

Wednesday, May 7

☐ AP Calculus AB Exam, AP Calculus BC Exam
(morning)

☐ AP Chinese Language and Culture Exam
(afternoon)

Thursday, May 8

☐ AP English Literature Exam, AP German Language
Exam (morning)

☐ AP Japanese Language and Culture, French
Literature (afternoon)

Friday, May 9

☐ June ACT, registration deadline

☐ AP U.S. History Exam (morning)

☐ AP European History Exam, AP Studio Art Portfolios
due (afternoon)

☐ American Fire Sprinkler Association Essay Contest.
www.afsascholarship.org

Saturday, May 10

☐ SAT and Subject Tests administered

More than one million students nationwide take AP tests every year, a hefty figure that has grown by leaps and bounds in recent years. AP courses follow a standard curriculum designed to be comparable to an introductory college course. The test is graded on a scale of 1 to 5, with a score of 5 roughly equal to an A in an introductory college course, a 4 equal to a B, a 3 equal to C, and a 2 equal to a D. Many colleges and universities grant credit for high AP scores, though some have become more stingy with it as the percentage of students who have taken AP courses has risen. With credit no longer a given, AP has morphed from a placement tool into an admission credential that serves as a proxy for the rigor of a student's curriculum.

AP tests are generally divided into two parts: a multiple-choice section and a free-response section that may include essays or problem-solving, depending on the subject.

AP scores can be reported to the colleges in the same way as all the other College Board scores. Each school gets a sticker listing a student's AP scores, which is often put on the back of the transcript. However, if they so choose, students can request that these scores be taken off the transcript and not reported. Students can also report AP scores officially via the College Board for $14, though this may not be necessary if the score is on the transcript.

Unlike the SAT and the Subject Tests, the College Board does allow students to officially report some AP scores and not others. Students are often reluctant to submit scores of 1 or 2 for exams taken in tenth or eleventh grade. But herein lies a dilemma: The high school transcript includes the AP course, so not submitting a score lets the colleges know that the score was probably low. For the most part, a score of 2 should be sent. Chalk up a 1 to having a bad day and don't worry about it.

The major competitor to AP, much less prominent in the U.S. but well-known abroad, is the International Baccalaureate (IB) program. IB differs from AP in that it includes the option of a comprehensive, two-year diploma rather than an a la carte menu of courses. For more information on IB, head to www.ibo.org. More on AP is available at www.collegeboard.com.

It is hardly surprising that most high school students have no idea what they want to do when they grow up. The real wonder is that anyone expects them to know. Our secondary education system does a reasonably good job of exposing students to English, math, history, and so on, and a terrible job of exposing them to potential careers. Ideally, classroom study of the liberal arts should be supplemented by consistent exposure to various careers.

> We began by visiting colleges during my son's junior year in high school. If we had a vacation or business trip, we would visit the colleges in that area.
>
> — University of San Diego mom

Parents, a savvy move is to help schedule shadowing experiences to explore career possibilities. If your student has an interest in architecture, see if you can help him or her connect with an architect for a day or a week of observation. If your son or daughter is interested in law, find out if the school counselor knows lawyers in the community who might be helpful. In addition to learning about a career, students learn about the world of work and get a chance to step outside their comfort zone. Spring break can be an ideal time, and many a summer job has developed from a few days of shadowing.

The Internet can also provide some valuable tools for exploring interests. At www.advisorteam.com, students can learn more about their temperament and learning style with a free interactive program. At www.profiler.com, students can take the well-known Campbell Interest and Skills Survey for a fee of $18. For resources on particular careers, www.collegeboard.com has a browsable resource area with extensive information.

There is no need to rush career training in the classroom. In college, liberal arts students do just fine in the job market while getting a well-rounded education. No matter what their interests, students can benefit from using extracurricular activities, internships, and shadowing activities to get a head start on finding a career path.

MAY 11–17, 2008

With APs in the rearview mirror, seniors are home free and juniors can breathe a sigh of relief (unless they still have final exams). The Class of 2008 will still find a handful of scholarships in play, notably awards from fifteen separate programs sponsored by the **Society of Women Engineers** worth up to $5,000 (renewable) and available to males as well as females. The weeklong **Step Up to Leadership** program is free for students who have completed ninth or tenth grades. (See Summer for Free, page 92.)

Sunday, May 11

_____

_____

Monday, May 12

☐ AP Biology Exam, AP Music Theory Exam (morning)

☐ AP Physics B Exam, AP Physics C Exam (afternoon)

☐ Society of Women Engineers Scholarship. www.swe.org

Tuesday, May 13

☐ AP Environmental Science Exam, AP Chemistry Exam (morning)

☐ AP Psychology Exam (afternoon)

Wednesday, May 14

☐ AP Italian Language and Culture Exam, AP English Language Exam (morning)

☐ AP Art History Exam (afternoon)

Thursday, May 15

☐ June SAT and Subject Tests, late-registration deadline

☐ AP Macroeconomics Exam, AP World History Exam (morning)

☐ AP Microeconomics Exam (afternoon)

Friday, May 16

☐ AP Human Geography Exam, AP Spanish Literature Exam (morning)

☐ AP Latin Literature Exam, AP Latin: Vergil Exam (afternoon)

Saturday, May 17

MAY 18–24, 2008

Late May is the time that students in the Class of 2009 should have a working list of about ten colleges. If you're still considering twenty or more schools, choices must be made. The time is at hand to plan summer and fall visits, and there is no way you'll be able to take a good look at more than about ten to twelve colleges. Dust off your college guides, surf the college websites, and narrow it down. One strategy is to combine colleges with similar characteristics and then figure out which ones you want to eliminate. Suppose your list includes roughly the same number of medium-sized universities and small colleges. If the small colleges on the list include **Allegheny, Bucknell, Franklin & Marshall, Gettysburg, Lafayette, Lake Forest,** and **Susquehanna**, consider the group as a whole with the goal of cutting two. **Bucknell, F&M,** and **Lafayette** are the most selective three—which of the three is your least favorite? **Allegheny, Gettysburg**, and **Lake Forest** are also comparable in selectivity. Is there one of these you can cut? By paring your list with an eye toward the big picture, you can ensure that you have a diverse and balanced selection of choices.

Sunday, May 18

_____

_____

_____

Monday, May 19

_____

_____

_____

Tuesday, May 20

_____

_____

_____

_____

_____

_____

Wednesday, May 21

_____   _____

_____   _____

_____   _____

Thursday, May 22

_____   _____

_____   _____

_____   _____

Friday, May 23

☐ June ACT, late-registration deadline   _____

_____   _____

_____   _____

Saturday, May 24

_____   _____

_____   _____

_____   _____

MAY 25–31, 2008

With no deadlines as May comes to a close, procrastinators in the Class of 2009 should hustle to line up a worthwhile summer agenda. The deadline for many summer programs will have passed, but many colleges will still take applications if they have space. Work is a perfectly honorable way to spend the summer, but rather than flipping burgers, try to find something related to a possible career interest, even if it means you must volunteer. The best idea of all may be to find a professional to shadow in a field of interest. (See Thinking about Careers, page 79.) For a rising senior in high school, a meaningful experience is more important than a few extra dollars.

Sunday, May 25

Monday, May 26

Tuesday, May 27

Wednesday, May 28

Thursday, May 29

Friday, May 30

Saturday, May 31

Preparation for the SAT is big business nationwide for outfits such as Kaplan and Princeton Review. Less attention is devoted to prep for the SAT Subject Tests, but the fact is that studying for these tests is likely to pay even bigger dividends.

Unlike the SAT, the Subject Tests cover a relatively limited amount of material. And unlike AP tests, which test a standard curriculum covered in AP courses, SAT Subject Tests do not always seamlessly match the curriculum of high school courses. Consider the Subject Test in U.S. History. Like all the rest, it is 100 percent multiple choice, with questions distributed relatively equally among topics from the American colonies to the present. But many high school courses emphasize some topics more than others, proceed thematically, or don't require coverage of a broad range of facts. Before you take any Subject Test, go online to www.collegeboard.com and take a peek at the sample questions there. If some of the material is outside the scope of your high school course, your best bet may be to buy a prep book.

As to choosing particular tests, the best approach is usually to stick with sequential courses such as math, science, and foreign language. Math Level II is the most universal choice for any student who gets to precalculus or the equivalent by eleventh grade. (Math Level I may be suitable for those in Algebra II or the equivalent.) A logical choice in science or language is generally the subject that the student has taken in eleventh grade. To do a foreign language Subject Test, students need to have a minimum of three years of study under their belts, though a fourth or fifth from middle school would be better. Since all but a handful of ultraelite colleges now require only two SAT Subject Tests, students have greater ability to focus in-depth on each test. (See pages 222–223 for the relevant lists.) Some students may want to get both tests out of the way in June; others may want to prepare for one in June and one in October. If the whole Subject Test thing is freaking you out, keep in mind that many schools will let you opt out of taking them if you submit a score from the ACT.

> Getting my application done during the summer before my senior year was incredibly helpful.
>
> —Colby College student

If procrastination has slowed down the planning for summer college visits, now is the time to firm up the details. The first half of August is the peak interval for visits at the nation's selective colleges—call well in advance for the best shot at an interview. June might be a better time to go if you have the flexibility. The crowds will be smaller, and more faculty and coaches will be in their offices.

> When you visit a college, try to arrange an appointment with a professor who teaches in your area of interest.
>
> —Valparaiso University student

The main drawback of a summer visit is that the real students will not be there. The hip-looking Frisbee throwers wearing the backward baseball caps are likely to be high-school-age impostors there for a summer program. A full-time student will probably be your tour guide, though he or she may not stray far from a spiel that the admission office has prepared. Look for unguarded moments of candor.

The key to a successful visit is to help your son or daughter line up as many points of contact as possible. The student should make the call and be as politely pushy as possible. An interview is option number one, unless the student is particularly shy. Admission offices say that interviews can only help you, and they're right. Ninety percent of it is just showing up and getting the brownie points for being interested. An interview helps the admission office put a name with a face—rarely does a student encounter an inquisition-style interviewer, though a few are out there. If the student hits it off with the interviewer, or gets on a roll talking about one of his or her interests, so much the better.

> Too often, students choose safety schools with a "hope to hell I don't have to go there" attitude.
>
> —Counselor's heads-up

If an interview is not in the cards, ask to meet with a faculty member in an area of interest.

Some academic departments have designated faculty members who handle this assignment. If this is not possible, option number three is an admission information session conducted by a staff person at the college. Anyone with a special interest—such as athletics or music—should also ask about coaches and directors and try to make appointments with them directly if necessary.

It is asking a lot for a seventeen-year-old to be the point person in making these arrangements. Parents should be prepared to step in and help when necessary, or to ask the college counselor to do so. Colleges will vary in their responsiveness, and you'll learn a little about how each operates. (For a comprehensive overview of college visits and interviews, see the *Fiske Guide to Getting into the Right College*.)

HIGH SCHOOL COURSES VERSUS THOSE AT A LOCAL COLLEGE

Advanced students seeking a challenge—and a pat on the back for going above and beyond—sometimes wonder whether they might be better off taking courses at a local college rather than their high school's honors or AP courses. In most cases, they won't be. AP culminates in a grade recognized nationwide, and the caliber of student at your local college may not be as high as in an advanced high school course. A college course is generally the better option only if a student is looking at specialized subject matter, such as a language like Russian or Japanese. If the subject is in the high school curriculum, the best bet is to take it there.

> Highly selective colleges are often not forthright about their admission criteria and seek applications from students who have little hope of being admitted. The reason is to keep the deny rate high.
>
> —Counselor's heads-up

June 2008

June marks the last round of SAT testing until October, with most students taking the Subject Tests. On test day, students are allowed to change their minds about which ones they wish to take, though students may not take more tests than they were registered for. The last ACT of the school year is Saturday, June 14.

Chemagination is a national essay contest sponsored by the American Chemical Society with awards determined at the local level. This week's deadline is for the national competition, but interested students must first enter locally. Head to the link below to find your contact. The National Foundation for the Advancement of the Arts sponsors the **Arts Recognition and Talent Search** (ARTS), one of the nation's most prestigious competitions for students in dance, film and video, jazz, music, photography, theater, visual arts, voice, and writing. Hundreds of one-time scholarships of up to $10,000 are available. The program is also the gateway to the **Presidential Scholars in the Arts** recognition program. June 1 is an early deadline with a second round on October 1. The **Donna Reed Performing Arts Scholarships** include ten one-time awards of up to $4,000 for students who excel in acting and musical theater. The **Sons of the American Revolution** sponsors the Rumbaugh Oration Contest, open to students in grades 10–12, which requires students to do a five- to six-minute oration related to the Revolution for scholarships of up to $3,000. June 15 is the state deadline; local deadlines vary.

Sunday, June 1

☐ Arts Recognition and Talent Search, early deadline. www.artsawards.org

☐ Chemagination Essay Contest. www.chemistry.org

☐ Donna Reed Performing Arts Scholarships. www.donnareed.org

Saturday, June 7

☐ SAT and Subject Tests administered

_____

_____

Friday, June 13

☐ SAR Rumbaugh Oration Contest. www.sar.org

_____

_____

Saturday, June 14

☐ ACT administered

_____

_____

TOP FIVE PITFALLS TO A SUCCESSFUL COLLEGE VISIT

5. Mom and Dad argue about directions—and the family arrives twenty minutes late.

4. Mom compulsively adjusts son's collar in the waiting room.

3. Dad decides he has a few additional questions after the information session; daughter turns crimson.

2. Mom asks tour guide if the dining hall food has enough roughage.

1. Son pretends he doesn't know Mom for the rest of the tour.

SUMMER 2008

IF YOU'VE FOLLOWED THE ADVICE OF THIS BOOK, you have scheduled a challenging and enjoyable lineup of summer activities. Balance is the key, so try to avoid overload and make sure you get a break from the rigors of school. That said, there are many things students can do in the summer to get a leg up on the hectic grind of twelfth grade. We realize that most of these are a pipedream, but here is the list:

- **Do a draft of a college essay.** Some students are lucky enough to attend schools that help them with essay drafts in eleventh grade. For those who don't, the summer is a great time to do a first draft of an essay. Students can take a peek at the essay topics of colleges they are interested in or write a general essay that could be tailored to various questions. One good strategy is to write the essay, put it aside, and then revisit it in October.
- **Do a résumé or activity chart.** Most applications ask students to write a list of activities, honors, and employment for their application. Doing it now helps avoid omissions and makes it easier to deal with the idiosyncrasies of particular application forms.
- **Prepare for standardized tests.** For students who were disappointed with their spring standardized test scores, the summer is a relaxed time to bone up for the fall administration. A few vocabulary words a night can help increase word power. Now is also a good time to take a coaching course that won't interfere with schoolwork.

- Work on the scholarship search. The admission process is work enough for the fall. Now may be the only sane time to identify possible scholarships. Many applications are downloadable online and can be completed in the summer even though they may not be due for months.

Grinding on college applications is not anyone's idea of a fun summer, and we would never suggest such a thing if not for the juggernaut that will hit in the fall.

Summer for Free

Families willing to cough up a few thousand dollars will find myriad summer opportunities. The list that follows is a sampling of the best programs that don't cost a dime. Because they are free, they tend to be competitive and therefore will add more teeth to a student's college résumé than a top-dollar Ivy League summer school.

We also offer a second list of programs that have historically been intended for students from underrepresented minority groups. These programs have recently come under legal attack for excluding white students, and some are now technically open to disadvantaged students from any background. Many colleges offer programs like these; we merely include a sample of the best and most interesting of them.

A third list highlights a few programs that, while not free, are low cost or noteworthy.

Open to All

Claremont McKenna College. Step Up to Leadership Program. Open to rising tenth and eleventh graders nominated by their principals, this weeklong program affiliated with CMC's Kravis Leadership Institute is free but does not include transportation costs. Claremont McKenna is a selective private college in southern California. Deadline: May 15. More information: www.mckenna.edu

Clark University. Summer Science Program. Students who are between the eleventh and twelfth grades can enjoy three free weeks of thematic science study at Clark, a medium-sized university in Worcester, Massachusetts. Deadline: March 1. More information: www.clarku.edu

Congressional Page Program. Students can spend a summer, a semester, or a year delivering messages to members of Congress—and get paid for it. Two four-week sessions for sixty-six students each are available in the summer. Students live in their own residence hall and get paid the equivalent of about $14,500 per year. More information: contact your senator or representative in congress.

> My visits helped me find out about things like class size and the number of teaching assistants, but most helpful was just seeing the attitude of students in class.
>
> —Harvard University student

Governor's School. The programs vary by state, and not all states have a governor's school. The schools vary in length and focus but are typically housed on a university campus. Most are free. For more information, contact your high school counselor or state department of education.

Massachusetts Institute of Technology and California Institute of Technology. Research Science Institute. Founded by Admiral Hyman Rickover, RSI is the nation's premier summer program for aspiring science whiz kids. The program lasts six weeks, and everything except transportation is free. Students who get in here can probably get in anywhere. Deadline: February 9. More information: www.cee.org/rsi

University of the South–Freeman Asian Cultural Experience at Sewanee (FACES). A two-week, tuition-free program in Asian studies. Prefers students entering twelfth grade. The University of the South (Sewanee) is a selective liberal arts college in rural Tennessee. Deadline: March 15. More information: www.sewanee.edu

Telluride Association Summer Programs. One of the nation's most prestigious summer programs. Six-week seminars focus on thematic issues in the humanities and social sciences. Locations include Cornell University and University of Michigan. Nomination required in

December. Deadline: January 16. More information: www.tellurideassociation.org

Wabash College. Opportunities to learn about business. Open to rising twelfth-graders, this weeklong program is ideal for students considering a business major. Wabash is a small, all-male liberal arts college in Indiana. (The program is co-ed.) Deadline: April 15. More information: www.wabash.edu/olab

Minority Students

Carleton College. Liberal Arts Experience. Open to students between tenth and eleventh grades, the program lasts for one week and pays for all expenses, including travel. Carleton is a highly selective liberal arts college in Minnesota. Deadline: Nomination by March 1. More information: www.carleton.edu/admissions/CLAE

Carnegie Mellon University. Summer Programs for Diversity. Offers six weeks of study for students in underrepresented groups who are interested in science and math. CMU is one of the nation's premier technically oriented universities. Open to students who have completed grades ten or eleven. Deadline: March 1. More information: www.cmu.edu

Massachusetts Institute of Technology. Minority Introduction to Engineering, Entrepreneurship, and Science. Offers six weeks of tuition-free study and all the fun of Boston in the summer. Open to students who have finished grade eleven. Attendees must pay transportation costs. Deadline: early February. More information: www.mit.edu

Quest Scholars Program. A small, highly competitive program that offers a five-week summer program and five years of subsequent mentorship to low-income, at-risk students. Based at Stanford and open to students who have completed grade eleven. Deadline: early spring. More information: questscholars.stanford.edu

> I reminded my son that for several of his colleges, the earlier he applied, the earlier he would hear back, and that appealed to him.
>
> —**University of Southern California Mom**

Telluride Association Sophomore Seminars. Six-week program open to African Americans that focuses on topics relevant to the black experience. Small and highly competitive. Nomination required in December. Deadline: January 10. More information: www.tellurideassociation.org

Noteworthy

Boston University, Institute for Television, Film, and Radio Production. Film is all the rage among today's students, and what better place to study it than Boston in the summer? This program costs a pretty penny—more than $4,000—but it offers a unique opportunity for students interested in film. Deadline: rolling. More information: www.bu.edu/com/itrp

Concordia Language Villages. Serving nearly ten thousand students per year, Concordia offers the finest in summer language instruction and is available for students in grades three to twelve. Languages include Chinese, Danish, Finnish, French, German, Italian, Japanese, Korean, Norwegian, Russian, Spanish, and Swedish. Deadline: spring. More information: clvweb.cord.edu

Eleanor Roosevelt Center at Val-Kill. Girls' Leadership workshop. A nine-day program for girls who will enter grades ten or eleven that includes a diverse assortment of themes ranging from citizenship to the arts. Requires a token fee of $200. Deadline: February 15. More information: www.ervk.org

> Often colleges "reconsider" financial aid awards. Private colleges tend not to match public costs, though we did have one family who asked and had Stanford match the in-state tuition of the University of Colorado.
>
> —Counselor's heads-up

Landmark Volunteers. Offers two weeks of community service in places ranging from Acadia National Park in Maine to Golden Gate National Recreation Area in California. Open to students in the summer after grades nine, ten, or eleven. Fee in the form of a tax-deductible $1,250 contribution. Deadline: March 15. More information: www.volunteers.com

Massachusetts Institute of Technology. Women's Technology Program. Not free, but at a cost of only $1,000 for six weeks, the WTP is definitely a bargain. Open to students after completion of eleventh grade. Deadline: February 1. More information: www.mit.edu

U.S. Military Academies. West Point, the Naval Academy, the Air Force Academy, and the Coast Guard Academy offer low-cost, weeklong programs that provide a taste of military life. Recommended for students who are considering the academies. Deadlines: early spring. More information: Contact the academies.

New York University, Tisch Summer High School Programs. Another pricey program that makes this list because it combines world-class arts programs with Greenwich Village in the summer. Need we say more? Programs include acting, dramatic writing, musical theater, and film. Deadline: March 10. More information: www.nyu.edu

University of Notre Dame–Summer Introduction to Engineering. ND offers this three-week program for about $1,000 to students who have completed eleventh grade. Other programs include an introduction to architecture and a low-cost weeklong program for Catholics that focuses on church teachings. Deadline: early spring. More information: www.nd.edu

SEPTEMBER 2008

WITH DEADLINES LOOMING IN THE LATE FALL, smart students will use September to get into high gear. Now is the time to double-check admission requirements and confirm the fall standardized testing schedule. Students with a first-choice college should consider applying via early decision and early action. (See page 105.) Students who plan to file paper applications should call or email to request them. By late September, students should make preliminary contact with teacher recommenders. Forms and backup material can come later. Families should confirm arrangements for September and October college visits. Students are advised to check with the guidance office to find out when college representatives are visiting.

WHAT TO DO:

✓ **Monday, September 8**
October SAT and Subject Tests registration deadline*

✓ **Saturday, September 13**
ACT administered

✓ **Friday, September 19**
October ACT registration deadline*

✓ **Tuesday, September 30**
November SAT and Subject Tests registration deadline*

*Approximate deadline. Check with www.collegeboard.com or www.act.org.

SEPTEMBER 1–6, 2008

The first meaningful date on the fall calendar is August 18, the registration deadline for the September ACT. This date is offered only in **Arizona, California, Florida, Georgia, Illinois, Indiana, Maryland, Nevada, North Carolina, Pennsylvania, South Carolina, Texas,** and **Washington.**

Most students have enough trouble keeping up with the admission process, but at the risk of overload, there is one other thing to keep an eye on: housing. Small private colleges are no worry, but at big public schools, the housing deadline often comes before the admission deadline. Consider the following, from the University of Texas at Austin's website: "Apply for on-campus housing as early as possible beginning at 6:00 A.M. Central Time on October 1." In other words, if you wait until 6:00 a.m. Pacific Time on October 1, you may lose out on the best dorms. Other places where it pays to apply for housing early include **University of Colorado at Boulder, University of Florida, George Washington University, University of North Carolina at Chapel Hill,** and **University of Wisconsin at Madison.**

If you haven't already done so, the Labor Day weekend would be a great time to get your testing schedule straight for the fall. The registration deadline for the October SAT comes next week, with the deadline for the October ACT close on its heels.

Monday, September 1

_____   _____

_____   _____

_____   _____

Tuesday, September 2

_____   _____

_____   _____

_____   _____

Wednesday, September 3

_____   _____

_____   _____

_____   _____

Thursday, September 4

_____   _____
_____   _____
_____   _____

Friday, September 5

_____   _____
_____   _____
_____   _____

Saturday, September 6

_____   _____
_____   _____
_____   _____

THE ANNUAL RANKINGS FRENZY

The beginning of school marks a uniquely American ritual: the release of *U.S. News & World Report*'s annual rankings of the colleges. The original version in 1983 consisted of a poll of university presidents. *U.S. News* has continued to revise its formula on a regular basis since then.

> For a West Coast "geo" applicant, we've found that Eastern liberal arts colleges are more accepting of early-decision applicants than those from the regular applicant pool.
>
> — Counselor's heads-up

College administrators continue to disdain the rankings—unless their college happens to place highly, in which case they hustle out a news release trumpeting the results. An important factor in today's rankings of national institutions is what *U.S. News* calls "peer assessment," a survey of presidents, provosts, and deans of admission wherein they are asked to rate other institutions. In a bizarre twist, administrators are now targeted by public relations campaigns from competing institutions hoping to curry favor for the next *U.S. News* survey.

On the plus side, the rankings give a good indication of the prestige and selectivity of institutions nationwide, and the regional lists can help families identify options that might have been overlooked. In the body of its college issue, *U.S. News* generally has better reporting, we think, than its major college-issue rivals produced by *Time* and *Newsweek*. But the numeric rank order should be taken with a full shaker of salt; there is simply no way to pigeon-hole institutions as big and complex as universities into a precise numerical scale.

The rankings frenzy would be comical if it weren't such a high-stakes game. A decline can send alumni into an uproar, while an advance can signal that a college is "on-the-move." Small wonder that the colleges form committees and conduct studies to find out what determines the rankings and how they can package their numbers to look better. As long as the *U.S. News* college issue keeps flying off the shelves, the jockeying for position will continue.

SEPTEMBER 7–13, 2008

This week's administration of the ACT will take place in only a handful of states, listed in Appendix A. At midweek, the names of about 16,000 **National Merit Semifinalists** are announced to the media, though most qualifying students will probably be notified a few days earlier by their schools. (See page 24.) Semifinalists have just under a month to complete their Finalist applications, which include an essay, grade report, and recommendation. Semifinalists must also take an SAT on one of the designated dates and send an official report to National Merit.

If you're going to need teacher recommendations, this week would be a great time to ask. Some teachers get swamped with requests, and asking early can move you to the front of the line. (See page 111.)

The PSAT deadline for students with disabilities applies to high school counselors, who must forward forms by this date for every student they believe deserves testing with accommodations. In order to get accommodations, students must have the proper documentation from a qualified professional. (See page xix.)

Sunday, September 7

Monday, September 8

☐ October SAT and Subject Tests, registration deadline (approximate)

Tuesday, September 9

Wednesday, September 10

☐ Public Announcement of National Merit
Semifinalists

_____

_____

_____

_____

Thursday, September 11

_____

_____

_____

_____

_____

_____

Friday, September 12

☐ October SAT and Subject Tests late-registration
deadline (approximate)

☐ Students with disabilities deadline to apply for
accomodations on the PSAT

_____

_____

_____

Saturday, September 13

☐ ACT Administered in some states

_____

_____

_____

_____

THE JEFFERSON AND MOREHEAD MERIT SCHOLARSHIPS

Not your run-of-the-mill merit scholarships are these. The Jefferson Scholars program is the University of Virginia's (UVA) premier competition, and the Morehead is a similar program at University of North Carolina (UNC) at Chapel Hill. Both are based solely on merit, and both cover the complete costs of attendance plus a summer stipend. Given that UVA and UNC are two of the nation's most selective public universities (especially for out-of-state students), the competition for these scholarships is somewhere between intense and insane. Both competitions are open to students who attend in-state high schools—Jefferson by nomination and Morehead by application. In addition, both programs allow nominations from selected out-of-state high schools with good enough connections to be included. Students not attending one of these schools have the possibility of consideration on an at-large basis. Whether or not you attend a participating school, don't even give it a second thought unless you have some heady credentials. The

nomination process takes place in September and October at the designated schools. Here are some other ultracompetitive scholarships that rival these, with the application deadlines:

- University of Chicago, College Honor Scholarship: full tuition, January 1
- Duke University, Angier B. Duke Scholarship: full tuition and summer stipend, January 1
- Emory University, Emory Scholars: up to full costs, November 1
- Wake Forest University, Reynolds Scholarship: full expenses and summer stipend, December 1
- Washington & Lee University, George Washington Honor Scholarships: up to full costs, December 15
- Washington University (MO), Danforth Scholarship: full tuition, November 1, nomination required.

THE EARLY GAME: TO PLAY OR NOT TO PLAY

Applying early is all the rage in college admissions. One recent study says that applying via early decision has the same effect as adding nearly 200 points to a student's SAT score, while early action gives the equivalent of a 100-point boost. Though Harvard and Princeton have eliminated their early programs, the tide of early applications is showing no signs of abating.

In early admission, terminology is crucial. Early decision (ED) entails a binding commitment to enroll if accepted. Early decision deadlines begin October 1 and continue through January, with some colleges offering two deadlines for ED consideration. Early action, a more benign program, gives students the benefit of an early yea or nay without the commitment to attend. According to one recent study, the advantage in admissions of applying ED is equal to about 200 points on the SAT, while the advantage of EA is about 100 points.

ED is controversial because colleges use it to manipulate their admission numbers so as to appear more selective. Students get the short end of the deal, losing about five months of additional time to weigh their options. ED makes sense for a student who is angling for admission at a "reach" school and who has no financial need. By throwing themselves at the college's mercy, these students have better odds of getting a fat letter. Students with financial need, or students who are confident of getting in, may be better served by keeping their options open and maintaining their ability to compare aid and scholarship offers.

Despite the pitfalls, applying ED will continue to make sense for some students. A few more schools may eliminate their early programs, but many more will keep them. If you're a borderline applicant to a highly selective school and don't need aid, consider it. Otherwise, be wary. For a complete analysis of early decision and early action, consult the *Fiske Guide to Getting into the Right College*.

SEPTEMBER 14–20, 2008

Ah, late September. The mornings are crisp, a hint of fall is in the air, and the sun still shines warmly. A perfect time to kick back and relax? Not if you're smart. There are storm clouds on the horizon called October, November, and December, and when they roll in, you'll be pelted with papers, exams, and application deadlines.

If you are lucky enough to have a late-September lull, use it. The last two weeks of September are a perfect time to get at least one of your applications DONE. Some hard work now will take the pressure off later.

Make sure that the registration deadline for the November SAT does not sneak up on you. The deadline is coming fast even though the calendar still says September.

Sunday, September 14

_____   _____

_____   _____

_____   _____

Monday, September 15

_____   _____

_____   _____

_____   _____

Tuesday, September 16

_____   _____
_____   _____

Wednesday, September 17

_____   _____
_____   _____

Thursday, September 18

_____   _____
_____   _____

Friday, September 19

☐ October ACT registration deadline (approximate)   _____
_____   _____

Saturday, September 20

_____   _____
_____   _____

SEPTEMBER 21–30, 2008

This week's primary deadline is for the November SAT. Many students use this date for one more crack at the Subject Tests after taking their last SAT in October. Even at colleges that don't require Subject Tests, a good score will be a plus. And one more reminder: Make sure you do some prep. Since the Subject Tests cover specific subject matter, the odds are good that preparation can improve your score.

The **Tylenol Scholarship** is one of the largest in the country, offering 20 one-time awards of $10,000 and 150 scholarships of $1,000 to students who plan to major in health-related fields.

Sunday, September 21

_____

_____

Monday, September 22

_____

_____

Tuesday, September 23

_____

_____

Wednesday, September 24

_____

_____

Thursday, September 25

_____

_____

Friday, September 26

_____

_____

Saturday, September 27

_____   _____

_____   _____

_____   _____

Sunday, September 28

_____   _____

_____   _____

_____   _____

Monday, September 29

_____   _____

_____   _____

_____   _____

Tuesday, September 30

☐ **November SAT and Subject Tests registration**   _____
  deadline (approximate)
                                                           _____
☐ **The Tylenol Scholarship.**
  www.scholarship.tylenol.com   _____

Much of the confusion in college admission comes from the fact that half of the colleges are trying to appear less selective than they really are, and the other half are trying to appear more selective than they really are.

Highly selective schools revel in their reputations for choosiness, but there is a problem. If students think that they have no hope of admission at the Princetons of the world, they won't bother to apply, and Princeton will lose applicants. Like all the other highly selective schools, Princeton wants borderline applicants to apply, not because significant numbers of them will get in, but because the fact that they won't get in will feed Princeton's aura as a highly selective school. If a typical B+ student goes to a session with a Princeton admission officer, will that student come away feeling as if he or she has a shot at getting in? In many cases, yes. Is it a realistic possibility? Probably not.

On the other side, consider Ithaca College, which recently noted on its website that "Typically, some 11,000 men and women apply for 1,550 places in the freshman class." Does this mean that Ithaca is accepting about one in ten applicants? Not exactly. In this passage, which appeared on its website under the heading of "Just the Facts," Ithaca left out the fact that it admits about 6,000 applicants in order to get those 1,550 to enroll. Ithaca is one of the many, many colleges that tries to make itself look more selective than it really is.

Rule of thumb: Assume that your odds for admission are lower than you might think after that wonderful meeting with the Princeton rep, and that your odds are higher than you would be led to believe from a session with an Ithaca admission officer.

> The admission process is about finding the place where you belong, not about portraying yourself in an artificial manner in order to be accepted at a certain school.
>
> —University of Kansas student

ROUNDING UP TEACHER RECOMMENDERS

Late September is an ideal time for students to contact teacher recommenders. But will you actually do it? Probably not. Students love to procrastinate on this one. They wait and wait—sometimes until the week before winter vacation—and then spring the recommendation request on a harried teacher who is already juggling ten other letters. Memo to students: You don't need to wait until you have all the application forms in hand to ask.

There is no great trick to getting a letter. An English teacher is the most logical choice—no subject is more central to a student's academic experience, and English teachers tend to be good writers. Alternatively, students may choose a history, social studies, or foreign language teacher. For balance, students generally combine one of these with a math or science teacher. Teachers from yearbook, art, or other non-core courses should generally be avoided. (If the arts are a particularly important part of your life, consider getting an additional recommendation from an art teacher to supplement the ones in core academic subjects.)

A teacher who can speak to the student's academic and personal qualities will typically do the best job. Some parents think they can work the system by contacting the close friend of their brother-in-law who happens to be on the board of First Choice U, or by getting a recommendation from the state senator who got a campaign contribution from Dad. By and large, these attempts at small-time influence peddling fall flat. If your family name is on the college library, that's big-time influence peddling, which will work just fine.

Students should be sure to give their teachers plenty of backup material on writing the recommendations. A note summarizing the student's experiences with the teacher—including references to particular assignments—would be helpful. (When teachers have one hundred students in their classes, it is possible to know a student well and still need a memory jog.) Copies of papers on which you did well would be a major bonus. An activity chart would also be helpful, and, of course, the necessary forms with the student's information filled out at the top. Schools vary in their procedures for mailing recommendations, but if mailing the letter is the teacher's responsibility, it is courteous to include stamped envelopes. Most important, students should emphasize the date of their earliest deadline and politely check back a week before to make sure the recommendation is in the pipeline.

WHEN ADMISSION OFFICERS COME TO SCHOOL

> **The essay separates the great kids from the nice, OK ones.**
>
> **—Counselor's heads-up**

College admission officers spend the winter and spring reviewing applications. What do they do in the fall? Many of them can be seen at a high school near you. Admission offices typically divide the country into regions, with particular staff members responsible for each area. Private colleges generally send representatives to all corners of the nation during the fall; public institutions usually limit their visits to contiguous states. Some colleges visit the same high school every year. Others will visit every other year, while still others hold group information sessions at local venues in lieu of high school visits.

Check in at the guidance office for a list of the representatives who will visit, and keep checking back because the schedule is subject to change.

Keep in mind that the representative who visits will probably be the first one to read your application. Even if the family has already visited the college and had an interview, students should make the effort to meet the regional representative at their school. Colleges count contacts, and the more a student has expressed interest, the better his or her chances are for admission.

Might a thank-you note be in order after the visit? Great idea—but few students ever write one. If you can't attend the session, write a note expressing regrets or get the representative's email address from the college counselor. Colleges know that students can't always get out of class—making the effort to follow up is what counts.

> **Always be yourself. Some of my friends got caught in lies trying to impress colleges.**
>
> **—Southwestern University student**

FOR PARENTS: TOP FIVE SIGNS OF A PROCRASTINATION EMERGENCY

5. Your son or daughter becomes testy when you suggest that four hours per day on the phone with friends may be too much.

4. Homework mysteriously becomes a top priority when you bring up the subject of college applications.

3. Son claims that he is spending three hours per night chatting with admission officers via AOL Instant Messenger.

2. Daughter refuses to discuss her college essay but insists that it is "almost done."

1. Son appears unaware that there is a deadline to apply for admission.

For procrastination coping strategies, see page 37.

OCTOBER 2008

OCTOBER IS WHEN EVERYTHING HITS THE FAN. Early applications at the most selective colleges should be filed by the end of this month. Students should complete their application lists and make a last check of their transcripts. Early October is the best time to firm up a game plan with the college counselor. Teacher recommenders should be confirmed. Financial aid applicants at highly selective colleges should complete the CSS/PROFILE where necessary.

The Class of 2010 gets a taste of the college admission process with the administration of the PSAT. For a less stressful way to stick a toe in the water, juniors should sit in on meetings at school with visiting college representatives. See your guidance counselor to find out the schedule.

WHAT TO DO:

✓ **Saturday, October 4**
SAT and Subject Tests administered

✓ **Wednesday, October 15**
Early-action and scholarship deadlines

✓ **Wednesday, October 15
and Saturday, October 18**
PSAT administered

✓ **Saturday, October 25**
ACT administered

October 1–4, 2008

October means that things are getting serious. The November SAT date is a close shave for early-decision or early-action programs, but scores from this date often get in there under the wire. **National Merit** semi-finalists must turn in their applications for Finalist by a high-school-specific deadline, usually this week. A letter of recommendation is required for each Finalist application, so don't be surprised if the college counselor has a slightly glazed look. The College Board swings into action with its CSS/PROFILE form, a supplement to the Free Application for Federal Student Aid (FAFSA), which is used by some selective private colleges. Students must register for it online. We recommend that students wait until their list of colleges is fairly firm before registering for the PROFILE. Since there are various questions that colleges require at their discretion, the form varies depending on where the student applies. The final deadline for the **NFAA ARTS** competition is also this week. The **Hispanic Scholarship Fund** teams up with **Toyota** to offer scholarships of up to $5,000 to students who attend one of six leading public institutions in California or Texas and major in selected fields. **Siemens Westinghouse** is a famous math and science project-based competition that awards scholarships that total up to $100,000 over four years. One unique program not on the calendar is the **Wells Fargo College STEPS Program**, which awards ten scholarships of $1,000 each month via random drawings that begin in October. For more information, head to www.wellsfargo.com.

Wednesday, October 1

- ☐ University of South Carolina, early action deadline
- ☐ CSS/PROFILE online application available
- ☐ NFAA ARTS final deadline. www.artsawards.org
- ☐ Hispanic Scholarship Fund/Toyota Motors Scholarship. www.shpe.org
- ☐ Siemens Westinghouse Competition. www.siemens-foundation.org

Thursday, October 2

_____   _____

_____   _____

_____   _____

Friday, October 3

☐ October ACT late-registration deadline   ☐ National Merit Finalist applications approximate due date

_____   _____

_____

Saturday, October 4

☐ SAT and Subject Tests administered   _____

_____   _____

_____   _____

It's really very simple. A college application includes four parts:

- **The student's section.** Includes basic personal information, a list of activities and honors, short essays about meaningful activities and/or why the student is interested in the college, and a more extended personal statement.

- **The secondary school report.** Asks the college counselor to evaluate the applicant with an essay and with check-offs about rigor of curriculum and personal qualities ranging from initiative to sense of humor.

- **The teacher recommendation.** A teacher's assessment of the student's strengths and weaknesses.

- **Test scores.** Generally reported from the testing agency at the request of the student, though sometimes also on the back of the transcript and in the student's part of the application.

Each section has a corresponding piece of paper (or two), and keeping track of these can be a big job. Online filers will submit the student's section electronically. A few high schools are able to submit transcripts and recommendations electronically, but generally students will need to print the relevant forms for the counselor and teachers. The counselor and teacher forms often have detailed check-off ratings that ask if the student is a) "one of the top few I have taught," b) "one of the best this year," or c) excellent (top 10 percent this year), and so on. But many school personnel bridle at completing these ratings and simply say "see attached" and clip their essay. A growing number of schools have designed their own secondary-school report forms and have dispensed with doing a different one for each college.

As the fall progresses, students should keep this in mind: The sooner they can get the appropriate forms to teachers and counselors, the sooner their applications are likely to be processed.

> The admission process seems more about the colleges and their "image" than it does about the student and the best match for them.
>
> —Counselor's heads-up

A Last Check of the Transcript

Parents and students have a right to see the transcript before it is sent out, and smart ones won't let the opportunity pass. First, check for mistakes, which are all too common. One hapless applicant to the University of Texas (UT) found out the hard way when he mailed his application and his counselor sent the transcript with an incorrect Social Security number. As do many large institutions, UT sorts applications by Social Security number. The transcript was stuck in la-la land for several months before the error was finally discovered. There are numerous questions students and parents should ask about the student's transcript:

- Does it include honors or activities? Some do, most don't. If so, does it include any the student has forgotten about?

- Are summer courses listed? The grade? Usually so, though awarding of credit varies.

- What about courses from previous schools? Has the school transferred all your credits?

- Which test scores are on there? Some schools report test scores on the back, others don't. Make sure the right scores are there.

The test score issue is particularly touchy because some students have scores they don't want to send. Some schools put the PSAT on the transcript—but if the score wasn't among the student's best, ask the school to take it off. AP scores can also be withheld at your discretion. If the student took both the ACT and SAT, one can be sent and the other withheld if the applicant so chooses.

Usually, a cumulative GPA is on the transcript, and schools have various ways of calculating them. Many weigh honors and AP courses. For instance, if an A is equal to 4.0 under normal circumstances, it might be worth a 4.33 or even 5.0 on a weighted scale. Methods vary. Some high schools omit arts courses from the GPA; many omit physical education. A GPA is meaningful only in relative terms, so don't worry about the boy across town who has a 4.8 at Crosstown High when the best possible GPA at your school is a 4.0. Bear in mind that many colleges recalculate GPAs according to their own criteria, and a few shave off ninth grade for a closer look at recent work.

INSIDE THE PSAT

The Class of 2010 gets its first meaningful introduction to college admission with the Preliminary SAT. Some schools choose to administer it during a school day—this year the date is Thursday, October 15—and others do it on Saturday, October 18. The PSAT is an abbreviated version of the SAT that many students will have taken once before as tenth graders. This time, the results count in the National Merit competition, which gives recognition and a chance at scholarships to just under 5 percent of the eleventh-grade test-takers. (See page 24 for details.)

In 2004, the PSAT underwent similar though less sweeping changes to those on the new SAT. The old verbal section was renamed Critical Reading, the analogy questions were dropped, and more reading passages were added. The Math and Writing Skills sections are largely unchanged, though the Algebra and Geometry sections will be slightly more challenging than in the past to better reflect the math that students cover through tenth grade. As before, there is no essay on the PSAT. (For more on the new SAT, see page 42.)

Unlike the SAT and ACT, the PSAT is a school-based test and generally students are automatically signed up to take it. If in doubt, check to make sure. Students who are homeschooled should contact a local high school and arrange to take the test there. Students occasionally have problems if their school arranges a Saturday administration that conflicts with an athletic contest or other event. Students are allowed to take the test at a school other than their own, and students with conflicts on Saturday should investigate local schools that may be giving it on Wednesday. Unfortunately, there is no way to make up the PSAT. Students who miss it can qualify for the National Merit Scholarship Competition with a high score on the SAT.

For Parents: Another Chorus of the Procrastination Blues

So you followed our advice in the spring and it didn't work, eh? Son or daughter is still in major denial and you don't know what to do? Don't panic, and try to distinguish between serious paralysis and the garden-variety avoidance that is rampant at this time of the year, even among high-functioning kids.

The surest sign of real trouble is when nothing is happening: Your son or daughter shows no effort to get applications, doesn't show up at college visits, and generally is not engaged in the process. If that sounds familiar, you're probably at wit's end about how to deal.

We can imagine the scenario. You suggest working on applications. Nothing happens. You say no more TV or computer until applications are done. Still nothing. You declare a lockdown until applications are done. More avoidance.

Clearly, you and your child are now at loggerheads. Any push from you will provoke an equal and opposite push back. Although your son or daughter may be wearing a mask of indifference, their real message is that the burden of everything—college applications, leaving home, figuring out what to do with the rest of their lives—has become too much for them to deal with productively. They don't need to be told what to do; they need active assistance in doing it.

Break the adversarial dynamic and become an ally. Help make a list of major deadlines. Sit down together and begin work on applications. You'll probably encounter some resistance, so be low-key but persistent. Help organize and set priorities but let the student do the real work. Once the ball is rolling, look for opportunities to pull back.

One other thought: Suggest a college visit with a friend. This can be delicate, but if a friend of your child is looking at some of the same colleges, encourage them to make a visit together or with you. Harnessing the benign impact of peers is especially useful for boys who have girlfriends. You may not want them going to the same college, but the chances are good that the girlfriend is much further ahead in looking at colleges.

We wish we could say that these strategies are foolproof—you know they're not. Procrastination is a tough nut to crack. If all else fails, remind yourself that everything will ultimately work out. Young people find their way in life through a variety of paths. Your child will be no exception.

October 5–11, 2008

Welcome to the last week of sanity before the final early-decision scramble. Anyone seeking help with applications or essays will receive a warmer reception in the guidance office this week than they will later in the month. Ditto for contacting teacher recommenders. If asking for a recommendation has, er, slipped your mind or if you have decided at the last minute to apply early, we recommend that you bring flowers or candy along with the form.

This week is also a good time to get serious about the scholarship search. Many require paperwork from teachers or the guidance office. Turn in forms and ask for recommendations at least three weeks in advance.

Early-decision and early-action applicants who plan to apply for financial aid at colleges requiring the CSS/PROFILE should register to receive the form at www.collegeboard.com and file by November 1.

The **Outstanding Students of America** organization bestows ten one-time scholarships of up to $10,000, with an emphasis on community service.

Monday, October 5

_____

_____

_____

Tuesday, October 6

_____

_____

_____

Tuesday, October 7

_____

_____

_____

Wednesday, October 8

_____

_____

_____

Thursday, October 9

☐ November SAT and Subject Tests, late-registration
deadline (approximate)

_____

_____

_____

_____

Friday, October 10

☐ Outstanding Students of America Scholarship.
www.outstandingstudentsofamerica.com

_____

_____

_____

_____

Saturday, October 11

_____

_____

_____

_____

_____

_____

October 12–18, 2008

Once upon a time, this week would have seen **Harvard** and **Princeton** applicants frantically trying to finish their early-action applications. Not any more. In September of 2006, both schools announced that they would abandon what the Harvard admissions dean described at the time as "early action hocus-pocus." But with hundreds of schools still offering early action or early decision, there is still plenty of scrambling to be done in the weeks ahead.

   Whittier College's deadline is for its Honors Weekend, when it parcels out scholarships worth up to the full cost of attendance.

Sunday, October 12

_____   _____

_____   _____

_____   _____

_____   _____

Monday, October 13

Tuesday, October 14

Wednesday, October 15

☐ PSAT Administered

☐ Whittier College Honors Weekend deadline. www.whittier.edu

☐ University of Georgia, Early Action deadline

Thursday, October 17

Friday, October 17

Saturday, October 18

☐ PSAT Administered

OCTOBER 19–25, 2008

D-Day for most early-application filers is around the corner. At the beginning of the week, these students should politely check with teachers and counselors to make sure everything is in order. (By Friday, the guidance counselor is likely to be in the middle of a stress meltdown.) On Friday, the CSS PROFILE begins sending reports to the colleges. Early-decision/-action applicants can use the PROFILE to get a read on their ability to qualify for need-based aid.

Sunday, October 19

Monday, October 20

Tuesday, October 21

Wednesday, October 22

Thursday, October 23

Friday, October 24

☐ CSS PROFILE begins sending reports to the colleges

Saturday, October 25

OCTOBER 26–31, 2008

If you think the odds are long at **Harvard** or **Stanford,** try the annual **Coca-Cola Scholars** competition, where about 100,000 students apply for 250 one-time scholarships of up to $20,000. The **Prudential Spirit of Community Awards** are only slightly less competitive, with a school nomination required to compete for sixty one-time scholarships of up to $6,000. The **Georgia Tech Presidential Scholarship** covers the full costs of attendance for top students who want to join the Ramblin' Wreck.

The **Horatio Alger Scholarship Program** offers one hundred one-time scholarships of $10,000 and another two hundred awards of $1,000 to students with financial need who have overcome obstacles.

Sunday, October 26

Monday, October 27

Tuesday, October 28

Wednesday, October 29

Thursday, October 30

☐ Horatio Alger Scholarship Program.
   www.horatioalger.com

Friday, October 31

☐ Prudential Spirit of Community Awards.
   www.prudential.com

☐ Georgia Tech President's Scholarship.
   www.psp.gatech.edu

☐ Coca-Cola Scholars. www.coca-colascholars.org

TEN SIGNS THAT THE COLLEGE RAT RACE IS OUT OF CONTROL

Parents aren't the only ones who get stressed out over the college search. By late fall of twelfth grade, the whole family may be losing its grip on reality. Here are some warning signs:

10. Son ignores State Department travel warning in order to seek résumé-building community service experience among Kurdish separatists near the Iraq–Turkey border.

9. Daughter complains that classmate who uses a wheelchair has better college essay topic.

8. Son is distressed to learn that the SAT does not offer extra-credit problems.

7. Mom has a sudden falling out with best friend after the friend's daughter is accepted early at Yale.

6. Dad proclaims that only SAT vocabulary words may be used in dinner conversations.

5. The family hires a private investigator to verify that the student's great-great-grandfather was half Cherokee.

4. Thanksgiving dinner conversation is devoted to critiquing essay drafts.

3. Daughter memorizes Tiers I and II of the *U.S. News* National University rankings.

2. Mom searches the Web for a car-window decal that says "also accepted at . . ."

1. Message on the family answering machine notes that daughter is a National Merit Semifinalist.

NOVEMBER 2008

PRIME TIME CONTINUES FOR FILING APPLICATIONS. Most early-decision and early-action deadlines are in November, and students should also file applications at colleges with rolling admission. (These colleges evaluate applications continuously and typically offer a decision in about one month.)

After filing applications, early applicants should log on to the college's website to make sure their applications are complete. After a quick breather, early birds should focus on filing additional applications. (See page 141.) Worksheets for completing the Free Application for Federal Student Aid (FAFSA) should be available late this month (ask in the guidance office).

WHAT TO DO:

✓ **Saturday, November 1**
SAT and Subject Tests administered
Early-decision, early-action, and institutional scholarship deadlines

✓ **Tuesday, November 4**
December SAT registration deadline*

✓ **Friday, November 7**
December ACT registration deadline*

✓ **Saturday, November 15**
Early-decision, early-action, and institutional scholarship deadlines

*Approximate deadline. Check with www.collegeboard.com or www.act.org.

NOVEMBER 1–8, 2008

November 1 begins the deadline season in earnest. Institutions with early-decision deadlines include **Boston University, Brown, Dartmouth, Emory, Rice,** and **Wellesley,** among others. Early-action deadlines are at **Caltech, Georgetown, James Madison, MIT, SMU,** and **Tulane.** Fifteen full-tuition scholarships are up for grabs to early applicants at **Boston College,** and **North Carolina State** offers sixty scholarships that cover the full cost of attendance. **Miami University of Ohio** has a November 1 deadline for its full-ride **Harrison Scholarship,** and **Rhodes College** requires a nomination for its full-tuition **Bellingrath Scholarship.** Other colleges with a scholarship deadline of November 1 include **University of Kansas, Michigan State, Scripps, University of Tennessee,** and **Villanova University.** (For a complete list of November deadlines, see Appendix B.)

The **VFW Voice of Democracy** competition bestows fifty one-time awards of up to $30,000. Students in grades nine through twelve may enter the competition with a three to five minute audiotape of themselves giving a speech. The **Susan G. Komen Breast Cancer Foundation** grants five one-time scholarships of $10,000 to students who have lost a parent to breast cancer.

Saturday, November 1

- ☐ SAT and Subject Tests administered
- ☐ Early-decision and early-action deadlines
- ☐ Institutional merit scholarship deadlines

- ☐ VFW Voice of Democracy Scholarship. www.vfw.org
- ☐ Susan G. Komen Breast Cancer Foundation College Scholarship Award. www.komen.org/grants

Sunday, November 2

_____

_____

_____

Monday, November 3

_____

_____

_____

Tuesday, November 4

☐ December SAT and Subject Tests, late-registration
deadline (approximate)

_____

_____

_____

_____

Wednesday, November 5

_____

_____

_____

_____

_____

_____

Thursday, November 6

_____

_____

_____

_____

_____

_____

Friday, November 7

☐ December ACT, registration deadline (approximate)

_____

_____

Saturday, November 8

ESSAY HELP: HOW MUCH IS TOO MUCH?

It was a sign of the times when Duke University asked applicants from the Class of 2007 if they had received help on their essays. (Ninety-five percent said they had.) Skepticism of essays written like E. B. White by kids with grades like George W. Bush has been growing in recent years. Was it Mom who wrote with such flourish about how you dove and caught the ball? Did Dad's secretary polish it up? Which ideas were the student's, and which came from the college counselor?

There is nothing wrong with offering help on an essay. Here are some perfectly legitimate ways for parents to assist:

- **Probing for a topic.** Some students have a hard time with self-disclosure. Parents can help steer them toward a topic they can make their own.

- **Organization, word choice, and grammar.** There is nothing wrong with flagging common errors, or suggesting that the student look again at how the piece is organized.

- **Proofread, proofread, proofread.** Students are anxious about writing their essay, and as a result they want to get it done as fast as possible. Many an essay is marred with careless errors. Parents should strongly recommend that the student show them the final draft before mailing it out, or that they set it aside and then proof it one more time.

So where is the line? We draw a bright one at the point where a parent becomes tempted to write the essay rather than simply raising issues and pointing out mistakes. If you find yourself composing sentences, take a deep breath and several steps back. For a complete overview of the college essay, consult *Fiske's Real College Essays That Work.*

November 9–15, 2008

This week's early-decision deadlines include **Barnard, Bowdoin, Carnegie Mellon, Hamilton, Mount Holyoke, Tufts,** and **Wake Forest.** Early-action deadlines include **University of Chicago, Colorado College, Pepperdine,** and **SUNY Binghamton.** (For a complete list, see Appendix B.) **Deep Springs College,** with its admission deadline of November 15, enrolls a grand total of twenty-five Ivy-caliber male students on a remote campus in the Southwestern desert. And at the head of a growing trend among state universities, **University of Illinois at Urbana-Champaign** has its priority regular-decision deadline this week.

    Army ROTC offers full tuition and books at more than six hundred colleges and universities in exchange for a commitment to serve after graduation. The **Intel Science Talent Search,** now more than sixty years old, was sponsored by Westinghouse until 1998. Five finalists have gone on to win the Nobel Prize. The Talent Search offers 340 scholarships to those who complete a scientific research project of not more than twenty pages. The grand prize of $100,000 is one of the richest of any contest in the nation.

Sunday, November 9

_____

_____

_____

_____

Monday, November 10

☐ Elon University and University of North Carolina at Asheville, early-action deadline

☐ Williams College, George Washington University, early-decision deadline

☐ University of Illinois at Urbana-Champaign priority admission deadline

☐ Intel Science Talent Search. www.sciserv.org/sts

Tuesday, November 11

_____

_____

_____

Wednesday, November 12

_____

_____

_____

Thursday, November 13

☐ December SAT and Subject Tests, late-registration deadline (approximate)

_____

_____

_____

_____

Friday, November 14

_____

_____

_____

_____

_____

_____

Saturday, November 15

☐ Early-decision and early-action deadlines

☐ Deep Springs College admission deadline

☐ Institutional merit scholarship deadlines

☐ Army ROTC Scholarship. www.armyrotc.com

_____

_____

THE APPLICATION: ONLINE VERSUS PAPER

In the days when computers occupied entire rooms instead of desktops, students spent most of the fall chasing down paper applications from the colleges where they wanted to apply. It was a fun little game: 1) Student called the college. 2) College said it would send the application. 3) Weeks passed, no application. 4) Student called again. 5) College said it would send application again. 6) Weeks passed and still no application.

A contingent of students still applies via paper applications, but the vast majority of students now send their applications with a key stroke rather than a stamp. The convenience can't be beat. Online applications are still usually printed out and read the old-fashioned way, but colleges prefer them because they are easier to process than the snail-mail variety. Many colleges offer incentives to apply online, such as a waiver of the application fee. The majority of applicants to state universities apply online. Applicants to selective colleges have been more reluctant to jump on the bandwagon, though their numbers are growing every year. Pitfalls of applying online can include:

- Potential loss of data due to a computer malfunction

- Inability to see the printed version as the admission office will see it

- The impulse to hit "Send" before the application has been thoroughly proofread

- The fact that transcripts and recommendations must be sent separately

- Inability to amend the form or include attachments

None of these issues represents a real barrier to a smart applicant. The most important thing is to print the application before sending it—four or five times if necessary to get it just right. Additional material can always be sent through the mail. The paper-versus-electronic dilemma is really about comfort level. Old fogies like Mom and Dad would probably still prefer to use paper, while the X-Box generation is happy to use the computer.

COLLEGE ESSAYS ONLINE: ANOTHER MORAL DILEMMA

Movie buffs remember the scene in Casablanca when Claude Raines was shocked—*shocked*—to learn that gambling was going on in Rick's Cafe. That motif has been updated by the various online purveyors of college essays who are fueling concerns that today's admission offices are getting the best college essays money can buy.

> Make it easy for the college rep to remember you. Have a résumé handy in case the rep asks.
>
> —Counselor's heads-up

Consider one such outfit that we saw on the Web. It doesn't just sell editing services or sample essays; it sells packets of essays written in response to the questions at particular colleges. Applying to Princeton? Get a packet of twelve successful Princeton essays. Want to write about your athletic experiences? Buy a packet of ten essays in which successful applicants discuss how playing ball made you . . . er . . . made them a better person. You can even buy a packet where various students explain the reasons why their families mean so much to them—a surefire helper if you can't think of anything good about your own family.

The tone of the presentation turns solemn on the subject of honesty. "We absolutely do not condone plagiarism and have not created this site to encourage such behavior," says the site in its mission statement. Hmm. We'll take that statement at face value, and we admit that the line between cheating and getting ideas can be a fine one. Students will have to follow their own scruples on this issue, but be aware that every year colleges actively sniff out plagiarized or partly plagiarized essays and put their authors in the reject pile.

NOVEMBER 16–22, 2008

The run-up to Thanksgiving is a good chance for students to catch their breath—or forge full speed ahead on applications. Students should plan to touch base at least once more with their counselor next week to confirm application plans and turn in any stray forms. Keep in mind how tight the December calendar will be: Counselors must file materials for all January 1 deadlines before the winter break. That leaves a scant three weeks after Thanksgiving to get everything done. Any student who decides to add an extra college to the list should inform the counselor posthaste.

Sunday, November 16

_____   _____

_____   _____

Monday, November 17

_____   _____

_____   _____

Tuesday, November 18

_____   _____

_____   _____

Wednesday, November 19

_____   _____

_____   _____

Thursday, November 20

☐ December ACT, late-registration deadline
  (approximate)

☐ Grinnell College early-decision deadline

_____

_____

_____

Friday, November 21

_____   _____

_____   _____

Saturday, November 22

_____   _____

_____   _____

NOVEMBER 23–30, 2008

November 30 marks the first regular-decision deadline at two of the nation's elite public-university systems: The **University of California** requires that all students apply by this date, and **Penn State** has its priority deadline. The **National Security Agency** and **Defense Intelligence Agency** offer renewable, full-tuition scholarships and internships to students in selected majors who agree to post-graduation employment. The DIA scholarship has an income ceiling.

Sunday, November 23

_____   _____

_____   _____

Monday, November 24

_____

_____

Tuesday, November 25

_____

_____

Wednesday, November 26

_____

_____

Thursday, November 27

_____

_____

Friday, November 28

_____

_____

Saturday, November 29

_____

_____

☐ University of California admission deadline

☐ National Security Agency, Stokes Educational Scholarship Program www.nsa.gov

☐ Penn State University priority-admission deadline

☐ Defense Intelligence Agency Undergraduate Training Assistance Program. www.dia.mil

THE COMMON APPLICATION CONUNDRUM

Available at www.commonapp.org, the Common Application is a form supported by more than 300 colleges nationwide who agree to accept it in lieu of their own form. Participants are overwhelmingly private, though a smattering of public institutions such as Miami University (OH) and University of Maine at Orono also use the form. The idea is to cut down on paperwork by allowing students to complete only one application, photocopy it, and then send it to all the colleges. In recent years, the Common App has picked up steam, with recent converts including Princeton and Yale.

Nevertheless, many high-profile institutions still do not accept the Common App, such as the University of Chicago, Columbia University, Georgetown, and MIT, to name a few. In addition, many Common App institutions continue to produce an application form of their own, though in recent years more institutions, among them Dartmouth, Harvard, and Middlebury, have chosen to use the Common exclusively.

When the college has a form of its own, is it better to use that form or is it OK to use the Common? The debate has raged back and forth. Common App schools pledge to give the applicants who use it the same consideration they give to those who use their own form. Yet some college counselors remain wary. Will college admission officers subconsciously favor their own form? Will they question the commitment of Common App applicants to their particular institution because it is so easy to reproduce? A high-profile dean of admission recently created a stir when he suggested on national television that he would not use the Common App if applying to schools that have their own form.

Despite qualms such as these, students who use the Common App get a fair shake nine out of ten times. Students who want to hedge their bets might apply to a first-choice college using its own form, then use the Common App for other applications. Students who use the Common App should take care to make contact with admission officers and visit the campus to show that they are sincerely interested.

COMBATING DEER-IN-THE-HEADLIGHTS SYNDROME

After pouring their hearts and souls into an early application, students often have glazed looks on their faces when the subject turns to working on other applications. Ideally, a student would kiss the early application good-bye, chill out for a week, and then get back to the task of applying to other places. In reality, many students freeze. Everyone hopes to get a fat letter in mid-December, but those who don't should have a backup plan that does not include chasing the college counselor down the hall with five more applications on the last day before the winter break. This is where parents can be a big help.

Encourage your son or daughter not to put all their eggs in one basket. Don't get fixated on one particular school, and don't let them do it either. Stay measured and cautiously optimistic. Once the early application is in, help your son or daughter focus on other applications.

> There is much more emphasis on test scores today, contrary to how colleges try to downplay their significance.
>
> —Counselor's heads-up

CHECKING THE LIST ONE MORE TIME

As the final application push begins, it is a smart move to take one more look at the application list. If the student has a first-choice college where admission is probable, the list may be only two or three schools. Applicants to selective institutions will probably want to apply to five to seven or so. Students should make sure that the mix includes at least two schools where they are likely to be admitted and at least one institution that the family can afford, with or without aid. Students who apply to two very likely schools are assured of a choice in April rather than being stuck at a lone "safety" school that may not be as appealing in April as it is in November. Most students will have no trouble identifying their dream schools, and as long as their bases are covered on the less-selective side, they should be encouraged to apply wherever their heart fancies.

It also makes sense to think again about the affordability angle. If money is an issue, consider adding a college or two where a merit scholarship might be in the cards. Sometimes these places get lost in the shuffle because they tend to be less selective than the "reach" schools that have the prestige. Students may crave being a face in the crowd at a highly selective institution, but they may get a better education at a less-known institution that gives them first-class treatment. Scholarship winners generally get the best an institution has to offer, including small honors classes, top professors, internships, research possibilities, and grooming for fellowships. Not a bad deal when you can also save money for graduate school.

> One college gave my son what amounted to an extra $3,500 discount per year—obviously a merit award, but called something else at this no-merit award Ivy institution.
>
> —Amherst College mom

DECEMBER 2008

NO MATTER HOW BAD DECEMBER IS FOR STUDENTS, the school counselor has it worse. Students should see the counselor early—and we emphasize early—in the month with a final list of colleges. About a week before the winter break, follow up with teachers to make sure that applications are on track. Students may use the first few days of the break to finish up January 1 applications. Financial aid applicants who sat out the early round should register to receive the CSS/PROFILE form where necessary. December is the last shot at the SAT and Subject Tests for most students, so make it a good one.

For juniors, January is the first recommended date to take the SAT Subject Tests.

WHAT TO DO:

✓ **Monday, December 1**
Early-decision, early-action, and institutional-scholarship deadlines

✓ **Saturday, December 6**
SAT and Subject Tests administered

✓ **Saturday, December 13**
ACT administered

✓ **Monday, December 15**
Early-decision, early-action, and institutional-scholarship deadlines

✓ **Wednesday, December 24**
January SAT and Subject Tests registration deadline*

*Approximate deadline. Check with www.collegeboard.com.

DECEMBER 1–6, 2008

Today's early-decision deadlines include **Drew, Earlham, Kenyon,** and **College of Wooster.** Early-action schools include **University of Connecticut, Goucher, Lawrence, Rice**, and **Willamette.** December 1 is **Boston University's** deadline to apply for thirty renewable, full-tuition **Trustee Scholarships**, while **Wake Forest's Reynolds Scholarship** covers up to the full cost of attendance. Other institutions with scholarship deadlines include **Beloit, University of Connecticut, Millsaps, St. Olaf,** and **Whittier.** (For a complete list of early-decision, early-action, and institutional-scholarship deadlines, see Appendix B.)

After years with a February admission deadline, **Marquette University** recently implemented a December 1 priority deadline for regular admission. The **University of Washington** and **University of South Carolina**, among others, now also have priority deadlines of December 1. The **Toyota Community Scholars** program offers one hundred one-time scholarships of up to $20,000 to students nominated by their schools in early December. **Air Force ROTC** offers renewable scholarships covering full tuition plus books to students attending more than nine hundred colleges nationwide. The **Society of Automotive Engineers** offers approximately one hundred scholarships, one-time and renewable, up to full tuition. The **NASSP Principal's Leadership Award** competition takes place each fall in selected high schools, and high schools must choose their winner by early December to compete for 150 one-time scholarships of $1,000.

Eleventh graders will be happy to know that College Board mails PSAT results from the October test this week.

Monday, December 1

- ☐ Early-decision, early-action, and regular-admission deadlines
- ☐ Institutional-scholarship deadlines
- ☐ Toyota Community Scholars. www.toyota.com/about/community/education/scholars.html
- ☐ PSAT results mailed to schools this week
- ☐ SAE Engineering Scholarship. www.sae.org
- ☐ Air Force ROTC deadline. www.afrotc.com
- ☐ NASSP's Principal's Leadership Award. www.principals.org

Tuesday, December 2

_____

_____

_____

Wednesday, December 3

_____

_____

_____

Thursday, December 4

☐ Oglethorpe College and Presbyterian College, early-action and scholarship deadline

_____

Friday, December 5

_____

_____

_____

Saturday, December 6

☐ SAT and Subject Tests administered

_____

_____

December 7–13, 2008

The second week of December is not pretty. Most seniors are staring down the barrel of semester exams and the final sprint to finish January applications. Many are also in suspended animation waiting for the results from the early round, which probably won't come until next week.

The final week before winter break is always a madhouse, so this is the time for students to politely check with teachers and counselors to make sure that recommendations and transcripts have been sent or will be sent. If applying for financial aid, get the paper version of the Free Application for Federal Student Aid (FAFSA) from the guidance office. If you plan to apply online—the quickest option that cuts down on errors—go to www.pin.ed.gov to get a PIN for you and one parent. Where applicable, register to receive the CSS/PROFILE via a paper form available in the high school guidance office or at www.collegeboard.com.

Sunday, December 7

_____

_____

_____

Monday, December 8

_____

_____

_____

Tuesday, December 9

_____

_____

_____

_____

_____

_____

Wednesday, December 10

☐ National Beta Club Scholarship. www.betaclub.org

☐ University of Southern California scholarship deadline

☐ National Academy of Television Arts and Sciences Scholarship Deadline. www.emmyonline.org

Thursday, December 11

_____

_____

_____

_____

Friday, December 12

_____

_____

_____

_____

_____

_____

Saturday, December 13

☐ ACT administered

_____

_____

_____

_____

DECEMBER 14–20, 2008

There is no use sugarcoating the week of December 15. Some kids will be winners and some will be losers as they log on to learn the fate of their early applications. (A few still wait for a decision letter in the mail.) Anyone with a heart hates this week.

The priority admission deadline arrives at **University of Minnesota–Twin Cities.** Early-decision deadlines include **Holy Cross, University of Puget Sound,** and **Wells.** Early-action deadlines include **Ohio Wesleyan, Trinity (TX),** and **Wabash.** A number of institutions have scholarship deadlines, including **Kenyon, Redlands, Tulane,** and **Washington & Lee.** (See the appendices for complete lists.)

The **National Beta Club** offers more than two hundred one-time scholarships of up to $15,000 to students who are members of Beta Club, which has 7,500 chapters in forty-one states and emphasizes service and leadership. The **AXA Achievement Scholarship** program, administered in association with *U.S. News & World Report*, offers ten awards of $25,000 and forty-two awards of $10,000 to students throughout the nation who have shown outstanding achievement in a nonacademic project. The **Burger King Scholars** program offers 1,500 one-time awards to twelfth graders who must work at least fifteen hours per week and have financial need. One student is nominated per school. The **National Academy of Television Arts and Sciences** offers two renewable scholarships of $10,000 per year to students who plan to major in a TV-related field. The **Hispanic Scholarship Fund** offers awards of up to $2,500 through its National High School Scholarship program. Other programs administered by the fund have various deadlines.

Sunday, December 14

_____   _____

_____   _____

_____   _____

Monday, December 15

- ☐ Regular-admission deadlines
- ☐ Early-decision and early-action deadlines
- ☐ Institutional-scholarship deadlines
- ☐ AXA Achievement Scholarship Deadline
  www.axa-achievement.com

- ☐ Burger King Scholars Program.
  www.bk.com
- ☐ Hispanic Scholarship Fund.
  www.hsf.net/scholarships.php

Tuesday, December 16

Wednesday, December 17

Thursday, December 18

Friday, December 19

Saturday, December 20

SENDING EXTRA MATERIAL

Along with the stress of completing applications, many applicants wonder if they should top off their applications with something more. Some pieces of art? A musical tape? An article from the school newspaper?

Sending extra material can be a good move, or it can be a disaster. Here are some guidelines:

- **Ask first.** If you have previously met with a college representative from a particular school, an emailed question about extra material would be a good way to keep the conversation going. Find out the guidelines for extra material. Some colleges toss out anything that does not fit in a 9" × 12" folder. Others farm the material out to a relevant academic department.

- **Do it in moderation.** You won't be needing that middle school science project that Aunt Emma thought was so special. Students should limit themselves to the one or two most impressive items, preferably produced in the past year. Choosing between similar items is sometimes hard but a better strategy than sending everything.

- **Make it good.** Realize that material in visual arts, performing arts, and journalism (to name a few) may find its way to an evaluator who is a faculty member in the field. Just because you have the nicest alto voice in the school choir does not mean that you will stand out in the context of national competition.

We know at least one admission office that has an end-of-the-year party where the entertainment is all the lousy tapes and videos that students have sent in. Most students who get into most colleges send only the application. Make sure that the rationale behind extra material is compelling.

It hurts when you don't get in early. Denials in March or April come paired with acceptances. In December, one decision is all that comes.

You know this is not the end of the world, but give yourself time to grieve. Parents, empathize but don't show too much disappointment yourself. Pep talks won't mean as much as modeling a balanced, realistic approach. This one did not work out, but others will. Colleges make decisions in the context of a particular group who apply for admission in a particular year. Every college and every year are different. There is an element of randomness anyway. Small consolation.

As soon as possible, students should set their sights on the work ahead—more applications.

Many students will not be denied outright, but will instead be deferred. Alas, the odds of deferred students getting in are generally low—significantly lower than the overall acceptance rate. Students with their heart set on a particular school can express continuing interest and update the college on new activities, similar to a waitlist situation. (See page 216.) But the realistic approach is, generally, to move on.

I participated in a Colgate online chat and it was the most useful thing I did. I was given the opportunity to talk with faculty, current students, and other accepted students.

—Colgate University student

DECEMBER
2008

Top Five Myths of College Admission

5. That students with straight A's and high SAT scores should get in anywhere. The sobering truth is that just because you stand out at your school doesn't mean you'll stand out in the applicant pool of an Ivy. If you get 700's and have a 3.8 GPA, that makes you an average applicant at Dartmouth or Stanford. Being average puts your odds at 15 percent or less, and that's before considering that most admitted students have a special talent or ability that puts them over the top.

4. That getting in is about strategy. Playing your cards right can help a little, but we're talking maybe 5 percent of the getting-in equation. Most college credentials can't be manufactured, and admission officers can see through the attempts of students (and their parents) to try to jazz up an unexciting applicant.

3. That getting in is about pulling strings. If only admission officers had a nickel for every applicant whose mother has a friend whose uncle is on the board of trustees. Don't be deluded by the idea that your close family friend can peddle influence. Unless your granddad gave the school a million dollars, you're better off applying on your own merit.

2. That college admission is a crap shoot. Admission decisions can seem random because high school students don't see the big picture. The goal of every college is to assemble a diverse and interesting class, and everybody who is admitted fills a role. The odds of admission at a particular school can change from year to year because both the pool of applicants and the college's needs change from year to year.

1. That the college admission process is fair. Life isn't fair, either. Just because you are good enough does not mean that you'll get in. The good news? If you apply to a sensible list of colleges, your college search will be a success, even if you can't control what happens at any particular college.

WINTER BREAK DEADLINE EMERGENCY

It is every counselor's nightmare to get a phone call on Christmas Eve from a stressed-out applicant. It happens. Maybe you were deferred in the early round. Maybe, after thinking about it, you have decided to apply to just one more school—and it happens to have a January 1 deadline. Remain calm. Do not call 911 or pull the fire alarm. The student should call the office first, then home—and be very, very nice about it. Most counselors are prepared to come in during the break to take care of odds and ends. Some may even be at school. Don't sweat it if you can't get in touch with the counselor. As long as your part of the application is sent by the deadline, the school's part(s) can come a few days later.

WHAT'S IN A DEADLINE?

As you're racing toward the post office on December 31, it may be comforting to know that most college deadlines are for postmark rather than receipt. With thousands upon thousands of pieces coming in at the deadline, it may take them several weeks to simply open the mail (one reason electronic filers can get their applications completed quicker). That doesn't mean it pays to wait until the last minute. A date of receipt is noted on everything that comes into the admission office. They know who procrastinated and who didn't. The odds of such a thing making a difference in any particular case are low, but colleges are aware that the students who get their applications completed early tend to be on-the-ball, go-getter types. Applications that are completed early get the first read, and they may be read more thoroughly than ones that squeak in at the last minute. This is nothing you can put your finger on—but food for thought.

And remember: Many deadlines for independent scholarships are for receipt, not postmark, and scholarship committees will not hesitate to disqualify applications that are even one day late.

DECEMBER 21–27, 2008

Ah, the blessed relief of winter break. With the fall semester now in the rearview mirror, the toughest grind is over. A few students may yet be staring at exams in January—not a pleasant thought. Many will use the winter break to finish off applications. There will be some procrastinators in the bunch, but for harried superachievers who run in ten different directions during the school year, the winter break can be a much-needed block of time.

The January SAT date is still available for the Class of 2009. Colleges with deadlines in January prefer the December date, but scores from January will get there in time. For students who took a December Subject Test and bombed it, January might give them another shot.

Sunday, December 21

Monday, December 22

Tuesday, December 23

Wednesday, December 24

☐ January SAT and Subject Tests registration deadline (approximate)

_____

Thursday, December 25

Friday, December 26

Saturday, December 27

DECEMBER 28–31, 2008

Whose bright idea was it to make all the application deadlines at the end of the holiday season? So much for family bonding. Maybe you'll get some quality time in the car on the way to the 24–7 post office.

The **Sons of the American Revolution Knight Essay Contest** offers three one-time awards of up to $7,500 to students in grades eleven and twelve based on an essay about the American Revolution. Essays must be submitted locally, and though deadlines vary by state, most are December 31. Visit the SAR website to find the contact in your state.

Sunday, December 28

_____
_____
_____

Monday, December 29

_____
_____
_____

Tuesday, December 30

_____
_____
_____

Wednesday, December 31

☐ Clemson University scholarship deadline
☐ Sons of the American Revolution Knight Essay Contest. www.sar.org

ART STUDENTS POLISH THEIR PORTFOLIOS

Students aiming for a program in the visual arts face a significantly different admission process than students in other fields, a process that can vary depending on whether they are looking for:

- An art program within a college of arts and sciences leading to a B.A.

- A B.F.A. program in an art school that is part of a comprehensive university

- A B.F.A. program in a stand-alone art school

Students should submit a portfolio in all three situations. However, arts and sciences students will be evaluated with others in the liberal arts based on grades, test scores, and so on, with the portfolio as a factor but not the whole deal.

Students going for a B.F.A.—a Bachelor of Fine Arts—will be competing with other art students primarily on the basis of their portfolios. Grades for B.F.A. applicants do matter too, simply because poor grades indicate a higher danger for dropping out, no matter how good an artist the student may be. All art students are strongly recommended to attend one or more portfolio-day programs in regional locations, where groups of admission officers from art schools nationwide come together to give students feedback on their work. The National Portfolio Day Association (www.npda.org) sponsors them in more than thirty cities throughout the country, and more are organized under local aegis. In addition to the work itself, the art of taking slides, photographs, or a video is also crucial because portfolios are generally delivered in those media. Each institution offers specifications for portfolio submission, which should be followed to the letter.

> When you visit a college, leave a note for your local rep to let them know you visited.
>
> —Counselor's heads-up

JANUARY 2009

FOR TWELFTH-GRADERS WHO HAVE DONE THEIR HOMEWORK, January will be a snap. Students can put the finishing touches on January 15 applications and add one or two more schools if they are so moved. Financial aid applications should be filed by the end of the month. Students who have been knee-deep in the admission process can use this month to refocus on the scholarship search.

Eleventh graders should begin the college search in earnest this month and plan for spring break visits. Now is also the time to think about a standardized test schedule for the spring. What combination of SAT, ACT, and the Subject Tests should you take? (See pages 49 and 83.) January is also a good time to give serious thought to summer and make advance arrangements when necessary.

WHAT TO DO:

✓ **Thursday, January 1**
Regular-decision deadlines at the most selective colleges

✓ **Friday, January 2**
February ACT registration deadline*

✓ **Thursday, January 15**
Regular-decision deadlines at highly selective colleges

*Approximate deadline. Check with www.act.org.

✓ **Saturday, January 24**
SAT and Subject Tests administered

January 1–3, 2009

The end of the application push is in sight for the Class of 2009. January 1 is the admission deadline at heavy-hitter national institutions, including the **Ivy League, MIT, Caltech, Duke,** and **Northwestern.** Binding Early Decision II deadlines include **Bowdoin, Davidson, Hobart and William Smith, Macalester,** and **Swarthmore.** (For a complete list of January 1 deadlines, see Appendix B.)

January 1 is also the first day that the FAFSA can be filed for students entering college in the fall of 2009. Families should do everything possible to secure W-2's and 1099's in a timely way.

Members of the Class of 2010 may seem like mere babes, but it is time for them to get serious about college admission tests if they have not already done so. Families should make a testing plan for the spring, which may or may not include the February ACT, which has its registration deadline this week. The **United Nations Association National High School Essay Contest,** open to students in grades nine through twelve, offers three one-time awards of up to $1,000.

Thursday, January 1

☐ Application deadlines at the most selective colleges

☐ Round II early decision deadline

☐ Institutional scholarship deadlines

☐ First day to file the 2009–2010 Free Application for Federal Student Aid (FAFSA)

Friday, January 2

☐ February ACT registration deadline (approximate)

☐ January SAT and Subject Tests late-registration deadline (approximate)

☐ United Nations National High School Essay Contest. www.unausa.org

_____

Saturday, January 3

_____

_____

_____

_____

_____

_____

January 4–10, 2009

The January 10 deadline list for regular decision includes **Elon, Georgetown, George Washington, Occidental, Rice,** and **University of Southern California.**

All but a few procrastinators in the Class of 2009 should be finished with their applications by this date. As students slide into the laid-back mode of second-semester seniors, now would be a good time to focus again on the scholarship search.

The nation's leading scholarship for minority students—the **Gates Millennium**—offers more than one thousand renewable full-ride scholarships with financial need as a factor. The **Ron Brown Scholar Program** is the nation's most competitive for African Americans. In a recent year, 8,500 students applied for the twenty scholarships totaling $40,000 for four years. The **Elks MVS** offers five hundred renewable awards of up to $15,000 per year, and financial need is a factor. The **Telluride Association** sponsors two of the nation's elite summer programs in the humanities—one open to all and one for African American students. Both are free. The **JFK Profile in Courage Essay Contest** offers one-time scholarships of up to $3,000 to students in grades 9–12.

Sunday, January 4

_____

_____

_____

Monday, January 5

_____

_____

_____

Tuesday, January 6

_____

_____

_____

Wednesday, January 7

☐ Villanova University and Santa Clara University, admission deadline

_____

Thursday, January 8

☐ Application deadlines at highly selective colleges.
☐ Discover Card Tribute Award.
www.discovercard.com/tribute.htm

_____

_____

_____

Friday, January 9

☐ Ron Brown Scholar Program deadline.
www.ronbrown.org
☐ Gates Millenium Scholarship. www.gmsp.org

_____

_____

_____

Saturday, January 10

☐ JFK Profile in Courage Essay Contest.
www.jfklibrary.org
☐ Elks Most Valuable Student Scholarship.
www.elks.org/enf/scholars/mvs.cfm

☐ Telluride Association Summer Programs, approximate deadline.
www.tellurideassociation.org

_____

"YOUR APPLICATION IS INCOMPLETE"

They strike like a thunderbolt in the night: Computer-generated letters and emails bearing an ominous warning that transcripts or recommendations are missing. Wasn't the school supposed to have sent that material weeks ago? At 7:00 A.M. the next morning, Mom is on the phone with the guidance office to find out what went wrong.

Usually, there is no problem. Colleges take a better-safe-than-sorry approach to sending these letters, often after the material in question has already been received. Here's an example. Suppose Alice is applying to Most Prestigious U. Her counselor, a virtuous soul, is working during the winter break and sends Alice's transcript on December 28. It arrives at MPU on January 3, is opened on January 6, and is entered into its computer system on January 12 (a relatively speedy timeline for January). Meanwhile, Alice applies using the online application on January 5. Two days later, MPU's computer notes that it has received Alice's application but not her transcript. On January 11, a letter is generated to Alice with the message that her transcript has not been received. The letter is mailed to Alice on January 14 and received on January 17, putting the family in panic city.

This is just one scenario. Many applicants get missing-credential letters. They are a routine part of the admission process, though each should be followed up on and resolved. Occasionally, material has been lost (by the college) or not sent, and there is almost never a problem with simply resending it.

> Be prepared to rewrite and revise your essay multiple times. I think I did mine about six.
>
> —Yale University student

Even when you know everything has been sent, it makes sense to keep following up until the colleges confirm receipt. Most schools allow students to check the status of their applications online—including updates on which items of the application have and have not been logged into the their computer.

WILL I BE COMPETING AGAINST OTHERS AT MY SCHOOL?

High school students eye each other nervously when they are interested in the same college. Since their schoolmates are the only ones they know who are also applying to "their" college, students naturally reduce the admission game to a head-to-head competition with Johnny Genius who sits in the front row in AP English.

It isn't necessarily so. Colleges do read applications by high school, but they almost never have quotas for particular ones. In one year, three students may get in from the same school; the next year, no one may get in. If one student is a math whiz and the other is a linebacker, they are more likely to compete with other math whizzes and linebackers than against each other. The same goes if one is the daughter of an alumnus and the other is a minority student.

Sometimes competition among students at the same school does play a role. If four students apply to Pomona one year, and the next year twelve apply, it may be harder to get in at Pomona for that particular year. But situations like that are relatively rare. With thousands of students in the applicant pool, a student's odds of admission are likely to be the same whether or not Johnny Genius happens to apply.

> We helped our daughter make a weekly to-do list in October of twelfth grade when it was clear that deadlines were coming fast and furious.
>
> —Washington University in St. Louis mom

THE PRESIDENTIAL SCHOLARS PROGRAM

Each year, in the month of January, about 2,600 seniors with stratospheric test scores will be invited to apply for the Presidential Scholars Program. Of these, about 120 will be chosen for an all-expenses-paid week in Washington to meet with public officials and attend cultural events. All Presidential Scholars receive a medallion courtesy of the White House.

JANUARY 11–17, 2009

The list of January 15 admission deadlines includes **Bard, Furman, Macalester, Oberlin, Reed**, and **Tulane**. Institutions with Early Decision II deadlines include **Colgate, Franklin & Marshall, Hartwick, Skidmore,** and **Wheaton (MA)**. (See Appendix B for a complete list of January 15 deadlines.)

The **Young Naturalist Awards** program gives prizes of up to $2,500 for outstanding science projects in biology, earth science, or astronomy. YNA is sponsored by the American Museum of Natural History. Students in grades 7–12 may enter. The **National Honor Society** sponsors state, regional, and national awards totaling $200,000.

Sunday, January 11

_____   _____
_____   _____
_____   _____

Monday, January 12

_____   _____
_____   _____
_____   _____

Tuesday, January 13

_____   _____

_____   _____

Wednesday, January 14

_____   _____

_____   _____

Thursday, January 15

☐ Application deadlines at highly selective colleges

☐ Early Decision II deadlines at moderately selective colleges

☐ Phi Delta Kappa International Scholarship. www.pdkintl.org/studser/sschol.htm

Friday, January 16

☐ February ACT late-registration deadline (approximate)

☐ National Honor Society Scholarship. www.nassp.org

Saturday, January 17

_____   _____

_____   _____

JANUARY 18–24, 2009

Members of the Class of 2009 should take advantage of the January lull to refocus on the scholarship search. Some deadlines have passed, but there are still plenty in February through April. This is especially true of local awards, which tend to have later deadlines. (See page 195.) The January SAT is absolutely, positively the last one that can be used for admission to selective colleges. Seniors should use this date only in a pinch—to retake a test that they messed up on the first time, or to make one final attempt at increasing a score that is too low for their liking.

Members of the Class of 2010 should look toward March as a likely time to take their first SAT. At press time, the College Board had not released the date of the test. Check www.collegeboard.com for up-to-date information. The registration deadline could be as early as this week.

The **DuPont Challenge**, open to students in grades 7–12, requires an essay of not more than one thousand words on a scientific topic for one-time scholarships of up to $5,000. The Telluride Association's prestigious summer program for eleventh graders has its deadline this week.

Sunday, January 18

_____   _____

_____   _____

Monday, January 19

_____   _____

_____   _____

Tuesday, January 20

☐ Grinnell College admission deadline   _____

_____   _____

Wednesday, January 21

Thursday, January 22

Friday, January 23

☐ DuPont Challenge Essay Contest.
www.glcomm.com/dupont

☐ Telluride Association Summer Program,
11th graders. www.tellurideassociation.org

Saturday, January 24

☐ SAT and Subject Tests administered

JANUARY 25–31, 2009

FAFSA and CSS/PROFILE filers should scramble to meet the February 1 deadline of most highly selective colleges. File on the basis of completed tax forms if possible, but don't miss a deadline waiting for a stray W-2.

Some parents may note that the FAFSA only allows families to send reports to six colleges—a bummer that has irritated families for years. Parents should file the form with the student's six first-choice schools. Then, a) when the student aid report (SAR) comes back, send a copy of it to the remaining colleges; or b) make a "correction" on the SAR by erasing some of the initial list and substituting the schools previously omitted. The latter strategy works because the FAFSA processor has already sent reports to the first list. However, this method won't work if you must make other corrections to the SAR, since any schools you cross out now will not get the amended report.

For this week's lone scholarship deadline, the **Discover Card Tribute Award** is among the nation's premier recognition programs for eleventh graders, with nearly five hundred one-time awards of up to $25,000. **Navy ROTC** offers renewable full tuition and books at approximately 150 participating universities in exchange for a commitment to serve after graduation. **Toshiba** teams up with the **National Science Teachers Association** to offer a contest for kids of all ages who work in teams to design a "technology of the future" for one-time awards of up to $10,000.

Sunday, January 25

Monday, January 26

Tuesday, January 27

Wednesday, January 28

Thursday, January 29

Friday, January 30

☐ University of Miami (OH) application deadline

☐ Navy ROTC scholarship deadline.
www.todaysmilitary.com

☐ Discover Card Tribute Award.
www.discovercard.com/tribute.htm

☐ Toshiba, National Science Teachers Association
contest deadline

_____

_____

SCHOLARSHIPS FOR LEFT-HANDED STUDENTS?

The come-ons are everywhere: "Billions in unclaimed aid." "Free seminar tells all." "Act now." Few facets of American life have been so thoroughly scammed as the scholarship search.

The old chestnut about scholarships for left-handed students is typical—a misleading myth with just enough truth so that it isn't an outright lie. This one was perpetuated for years by a popular scholarship guide, and by talk-show producers chasing an oddball story. It turns out that the scholarship for left-handed students is an institutional award at tiny Juniata College. It is available only to returning students and only to those who show financial need. Maximum amount: $1,500.

More ominous are the pitches that come in the mail for seminars in which the secrets of free money for college will presumably be revealed.

Typically, these outfits rent space in a local hotel or conference facility. They start out talking about money for college and end up with a sales pitch for financial services that you don't want to buy. The Federal Trade Commission has attempted to nail some of these organizations, which typically skirt truth-in-advertising laws. Learn more about scholarship scams at www.ftc.gov.

Smart families never pay anything for scholarship search services. The best scholarship search vehicle on the Web, www.fastweb.com, is free.

Another rule to keep in mind: Nearly 95 percent of all money for college comes via the institution where the student enrolls (including most federal aid). For anyone trying to find a scholarship, the first places to look are the colleges where the student will apply.

Few things are more shrouded in mystery than what admission officers do behind closed doors. The reality isn't particularly glamorous and can be summarized in three words: read, read, read.

> We talked to our daughter about why she procrastinated. Sometimes, there was stuff she was afraid to do. We tried to help her find good ways to approach these things.
>
> —Stanford University mom

Once an application is complete, it goes to a first reader, generally the regional representative who visited the high school in the fall. Admission officers (AOs) have a quota of applications they must evaluate every day that runs into the dozens, making for a lot of late nights in February and March. In about ten minutes, a seasoned AO can read the application, essays, transcripts, recommendations, and anything else that may be part of a file. The AO generally gives each file a rating—often two or more ratings for academic and personal qualities. High ratings mean admit and low ones mean deny. Typically, the file is then passed to a second reader. If the second reader agrees with the ratings of the first, and if those ratings point to clear admission or denial, the file will be processed or sent to the dean for approval of the decision. People such as coaches and alumni directors also have a major say in the process; any student who is on their short list has a big advantage.

Borderline applicants are fought over in committee, with each regional representative making the case for those from his or her area. This is when it can get ugly. At the most competitive schools, AOs often have to go back and cut out applicants who were initially on the admit list to get the class down to size. The full committee, generally including all the admission officers plus some faculty readers, will have representatives from all corners of the college who will go toe-to-toe for applicants who strike a chord with them.

One of the biggest myths is that admission offices are looking for well-rounded applicants. There is nothing wrong with being well-rounded, but the most compelling candidates generally have one or two passions that can contribute to a well-rounded class. For a complete overview of how colleges choose applicants, see the *Fiske Guide to Getting into the Right College*.

FEBRUARY 2009

SENIORS SHOULD FOLLOW UP ON APPLICATIONS via the Internet to make sure they are complete. Most financial aid deadlines are this month. Financial aid filers should watch for correspondence through the mail (paper filers) or online (electronic filers). Verify that information is correct. Families with special financial circumstances should contact the colleges directly. (See page 187.) Juniors should continue researching colleges and meet with college counselors where possible. Register for the March SAT and/or the April ACT where applicable. Families should solidify plans for college visits during spring break and continue weighing summer options.

WHAT TO DO:

✓ **Sunday, February 1**
Application and financial aid deadlines at moderately selective colleges

✓ **Saturday, February 7**
ACT administered

✓ **Sunday, February 15**
Application and financial aid deadlines at moderately selective colleges

✓ **Friday, February 27**
April ACT registration deadline*

*Approximate deadline. Check with www.act.org.

FEBRUARY 1–7, 2009

February 1 is deadline day at many moderately selective private colleges (and some very selective public ones) including **Franklin & Marshall, University of San Francisco, Sweet Briar, SUNY Geneseo, University of Wisconsin at Madison,** and **Wofford.** (For a complete list, see the appendices.) February 1 is also deadline day for financial aid applications at highly selective institutions.

For raw numbers of scholarships, the **Sam Walton** (of Wal-Mart fame) is probably the nation's largest, offering more than six thousand one-time awards of $1,000. **Junior Achievement,** an organization that promotes business and economic literacy in schools, awards a range of scholarships with February 1 deadlines. The DAR, **Daughters of the American Revolution,** also offers a range of scholarships related to U.S. history, government, economics, historic preservation, and health professions. The **U.S. Institute of Peace** essay contest is one of the best known of its kind, with more than fifty one-time scholarships of up to $10,000. The **Phi Delta Kappa** scholarship offers one-time scholarships of up to $5,000 to prospective education majors.

The **Minority Introduction to Engineering, Entrepreneurship, and Science** is a tuition-free, six-week program for minority students and disadvantaged non-minorities. The **Women's Technology Program** at MIT is a magnet for the nation's top female students and a bargain at $1,000 for six weeks. (See Summer for Free, page 92.)

Sunday, February 1

- ☐ Application deadlines at moderately selective colleges
- ☐ Financial aid application deadlines at highly selective private colleges
- ☐ Announcement of National Merit Finalists
- ☐ Sam Walton Community Scholarship. www.walmartfoundation.org
- ☐ Junior Achievement Scholarships. www.ja.org
- ☐ DAR Scholarships. www.dar.org
- ☐ National Peace Essay Contest. www.usip.org/ed/npec/index.html
- ☐ MIT Research Science Institute. www.mit.edu
- ☐ Women's Technology Program. www.mit.edu
- ☐ Phi Delta Kappa International Scholarships. www.pdkontl.org/studser/sschol.htm

Monday, February 2

☐ MIT Minority Introduction to Engineering,
Entrepreneurship, and Science Summer Program.
web.mit.edu/mites/www

Wednesday, February 3

_____

_____

_____

Wednesday, February 4

_____

_____

_____

Thursday, February 5

_____

_____

_____

Friday, February 6

_____

_____

_____

Saturday, February 7

☐ ACT administered

_____

_____

FEBRUARY 8–14, 2009

This week includes the deadline for a third of MIT's high-powered summer programs for students who have completed eleventh grade. The Research Science Institute is a small, elite program that attracts some of the nation's top technically oriented students. (The program recently expanded to include an additional session at Caltech.) The **American Foreign Service Association** offers merit awards of up to $2,5000 and need-based awards of up to $3,500, as well as an award for the best essay in its competition. The **National Federation of Independent Business** makes more than 400 awards of $1,000.

Sunday, February 8

_____   _____

_____   _____

Monday, February 9

_____   _____

_____   _____

Tuesday, February 10

☐ NFIB Young Entrepreneur Awards.   _____
  www.nfib.com
                                      _____

_____

Wednesday, February 11

☐ American Foreign Service Association Scholarship.
www.afsa.org

_____

Thursday, February 12

Friday, February 13

Saturday, February 14

☐ Research Science Institute deadline.
www.cee.org/rsi

Is There a Prep School Advantage?

The psychology of college admission plays interesting tricks. Just ask a student or parent from an elite boarding school how the process works. They'll tell you that the deck is stacked against East Coast prep schools. Public school kids, they say, can get a 4.0 GPA with no sweat while students at prep schools must scratch and claw for a 3.0. And with more of the smart kids concentrated in places like Connecticut and Massachusetts, the competition is much tougher for them than for students in, say, Indiana.

On the other hand, a public school parent from the Heartland may be thoroughly convinced that students at fancy private schools have the inside track at Harvard or Yale. The nation's top prep schools can get ten or more students into places like those in a single year; the typical public school may not see a student admitted in ten years.

The truth lies somewhere in the middle. Colleges always say that they evaluate students in the context of their school. The colleges make it their business to know how grading patterns vary from place to place. East Coast residents do have a harder time getting into East Coast colleges—more because of the colleges' desire for geographic diversity than anything else. At the ultra-competitive colleges, it is true that the top student at a no-name high school in Arkansas has a better shot than students in the middle of the pack at Milton Academy or Exeter.

But students at top private schools and savvy suburban publics get better college counseling than their peers elsewhere. They know how to play the angles, such as early decision, and counselors at high falutin' schools do have a degree of pull when the chips are down. (See page 193.) Some colleges will admit a student simply because he or she is from a certain high school—hoping that more students will follow. Students from lesser-known schools also have more pressure on them when it comes to standardized tests. A transcript from a prominent high school speaks for itself, but students from remote schools may need high standardized test scores to confirm their A's.

Students from all backgrounds get into top colleges. But with applications rising and acceptance rates shrinking, more are also feeling the pain of rejection. To these students, the process rarely seems fair.

Surviving the Audition

Students who think that an interview is scary ought to try their hand at an audition. The best high school performers in music and drama are old pros at producing under pressure, but the audition raises the stakes to a new level. Auditions are a one-shot deal in front of admission officers and faculty that make or break admission chances.

Scheduling is crucial for auditions, especially when students are applying to a number of institutions. Pay careful attention to how each college or conservatory spells out its guidelines. Some have dates or windows of time in which students are expected to come to campus. Others have regional auditions at off-campus locations. Coordinating these schedules and following up can be a headache, and admission offices for music and drama programs tend not to be as organized as those for, say, accounting. Stay on top of them and call to confirm your schedule.

The right choice of a piece(s) to act, play, or sing in the audition can be the most crucial ingredient of success. Applicants should make sure that they understand each college's guidelines and then consult with someone, such as a teacher or coach, who can give them expert advice.

FEBRUARY 15–21, 2009

Colleges and universities with February 15 application deadlines include private institutions such as **Allegheny, Rollins, St. Lawrence University,** and **Texas Christian University,** and public institutions such as **University of Kentucky** and the **College of New Jersey.** (See the appendices for a complete list.)

U.S.A. Funds offers one-time scholarships of up to $1,500 to minority students with financial need. For the Class of 2010, the **Girls' Leadership Workshop** offers nine days of programming at Val-Kill, the one-time rural getaway cottage of Eleanor Roosevelt, who is the inspiration for the program. The registration fee is only $500.

The *USA Today* **All-Academic Team** provides one-time awards of $2,500 to twenty students who are nominated by their schools. The April ACT date is the preferred spring alternative at many high schools, though some students decide to wait until June when school is out.

Sunday, February 15

☐ Application deadlines at moderately selective colleges

☐ Financial aid deadlines at moderately selective private colleges and public universities

☐ Girls' Leadership Workshop at Val-Kill application deadline. www.ervk.org

☐ U.S.A. Funds Access to Education Scholarship. www.usafunds.org

Monday, February 16

_____   _____

_____   _____

Tuesday, February 17

_____   _____

_____   _____

Wednesday, February 18

Thursday, February 19

Friday, February 20

☐ *USA Today* All-Academic Team. School nomination required. www.usatoday.com.

Saturday, February 21

FEBRUARY 22–28, 2009

With the third quarter coming to a close in most schools, now is a good time for students to put their noses to the grindstone. We're not talking so much to the juniors, who may already have a nervous eye on upcoming AP tests. It is the Class of 2009 that we're worried about, those erstwhile super-achievers who have been magically transformed into slackers by second-semester senioritis. They'll deny it up and down—but we know better.

A little easing up is not a bad thing. The students who fall into a coma are the ones we are worried about. Colleges have been known to rescind offers of admission to kids who do a big-time nosedive. B's and even an occasional C on the final transcript are unlikely to cause a problem, but students who get several C's or a D will have some explaining to do. Two D's or an F could spell serious trouble. Why risk it? Third-quarter grades don't go to the colleges (except in waitlist situations) so anyone who is at risk still has time to pull up their grades in the fourth quarter.

The **Optimist International Essay Contest,** open to students in grades 9–12, features one-time scholarships of up to $5,000. Check with local Optimist Clubs for deadlines.

Parents of twelfth-grade financial aid filers are advised to make sure that their applications are on track. Families should have received a copy of the FAFSA student aid report (SAR) and a similar document from the CSS/PROFILE, either electronically or through the mail.

Sunday, February 22

_____   _____
_____   _____
_____   _____

Monday, February 23

_____   _____
_____   _____
_____   _____

Tuesday, February 24

_____   _____
_____   _____
_____   _____

Wednesday, February 25

_____   _____
_____   _____
_____   _____

Thursday, February 26

_____   _____

_____   _____

_____   _____

Friday, February 27

☐ April ACT, registration deadline (approximate)   _____

_____   _____

_____   _____

Saturday, February 28

_____   _____

_____   _____

_____   _____

RED FLAGS FROM THE ADMISSION OFFICE

Most admission officers treat their applicants with the utmost professionalism. Yet at least half of all AOs are in their early twenties, and intentionally or not, they do make mistakes. Here are a few common ones:

- **Saying test scores are no big deal.** Some admission officers have convinced themselves that standardized test scores don't matter. They're humanists, after all. But the fact is that test scores do matter—a lot. The transcript is the most important factor in admission, but among students who have strong transcripts, test scores play a significant role.

- **Encouraging unrealistic applicants.** One of an admission officer's main jobs is to generate applications, whether or not those applications are from admissible applicants. Students who don't have a prayer of getting in can still have "great" interviews. For a reality check, head to your college counselor.

- **Asking students to name their first choice.** It is natural for admission officers to be curious about how their school rates on the student's priority list. But AOs are going too far if they press students to name all their college choices and/or which one is the top choice. Students should politely demur.

- **Encouraging early decision.** Admission officers may note that students have a better chance of admission if they apply early, but they should not cross the line of urging students to apply ED. The idea to apply ED should come from the student's head and nowhere else.

- **Pressing for a commitment.** According to the National Association for College Admission Counseling (NACAC), students should have until May 1 to make up their minds about where to go without financial penalty (unless they applied ED). Some colleges try to force students into a commitment before that date. If it happens to you, get the school counselor involved.

Most families can get a fair shake in the world of financial aid by filing the FAFSA, and where necessary, the CSS/PROFILE and/or the college's own financial aid form. (The PROFILE has additional supplements for noncustodial parents and those who are self-employed.) But some families have circumstances that beg further explanation. In such cases, there is no substitute for making your case to each aid office with a one- to two-page letter and supporting documentation. Among the usual scenarios:

- **An expected decline in earnings.** If your income was more last year than it will be this year, explain why. Include pay stubs if relevant. Be aware that if your income projection for the current year turns out to be low, the aid office will remember that when making its award the following year.

- **Unusual expenses.** If you're caring for Mom's father, or have health problems yourself that have recently cropped up, spell them out. Credit card debt doesn't count.

- **Self-employment.** For good or ill, financial aid officers tend to view self-employed people with a skeptical eye, particularly if you have high revenue and high write-offs. If you're not making as much money as your cash flow would indicate, explain why.

- **Uncooperative noncustodial parent.** Many a student loses out in the aid process because the noncustodial parent won't help. Some aid offices will give you the benefit of the doubt if the divorce was a long time ago and the noncustodial parent has no role in the student's life.

I had a student who was given a significantly better aid package from Harvard than from Princeton. Since his first choice was Princeton, I faxed his Harvard package to the Princeton financial aid people and they quickly matched the Harvard offer.

—Counselor's heads-up

"WINK LETTERS" BRIGHTEN FEBRUARY SPIRITS

In late February or early March, a few lucky students get an attitude adjustment from the colleges in the form of a "wink letter." These are friendly little notes to see how the students are doing and to say that, by the way, they're probably in. Nothing official, just a heads-up. A sample of the colleges that have sent such letters to top applicants in recent years includes Clark, Cornell, Dartmouth, Duke, Grinnell, and Smith. Colleges mail these as an attempt to get a foot in the door with students who will probably have other options when the acceptance letters are mailed. No one should be upset if they don't get such a letter from these or other institutions; many students will be admitted who don't get one. Those who do receive one have the satisfaction of knowing that they are now the ones being pursued.

> One family seeking more financial aid chose to fly out to the college (four-thousand-mile round trip) to plead their case. Two members of the family went out. The cost of the trip undercut the family's message of dire financial straits.
>
> —Counselor's heads-up

MARCH 2009

DECISION LETTERS FOR THE CLASS OF 2009 will come in at an accelerating pace as the month progresses. Families should scrutinize aid packages and make plans for final college visits in April.

Juniors should use spring break for college visits and/or to prepare for standardized tests. Students in AP courses should make sure they are registered to take the exam.

WHAT TO DO:

✓ **Sunday, March 1**
Admission and financial aid deadlines at moderately selective colleges; SAT administered

✓ **Saturday, March 14**
SAT administered

✓ **Sunday, March 15**
Admission and financial aid deadlines at moderately selective colleges

✓ **Tuesday, March 31**
May SAT and Subject Tests registration deadline*

*Approximate deadline. Check with www.collegeboard.com.

MARCH 1–7, 2009

Admission deadlines at moderately selective institutions continue today, including **Austin College, Hampden-Sydney, Ohio Wesleyan**, and **Purdue.** (See the appendices for a complete list.)

Kaplan's "My Turn" Essay Contest gives entrants in grades 9–12 a shot at seeing their work in *Newsweek*'s feature by the same name as well as one-time awards of up to $5,000. The week's other essay contest, sponsored by the **American Foreign Service** and also open to grades 9–12, offers one-time awards of up to $2,500. The **Pfizer Epilepsy Scholarship Award,** offering awards up to $3,000, is among the most prominent awards available to students with a particular medical condition. The **Department of Agriculture 1890 scholarship** offers renewable full-boat awards to students looking at historically black colleges. All-around academic and athletic excellence is the standard for the **Student Athlete Milk Mustache of the Year Award,** which echoes the popular advertising campaign with the same theme. Twenty-five one-time scholarships of $7,500 are available.

Carleton College offers one of the nation's premier summer programs for minority students, the **Liberal Arts Experience.** The program is open to students between tenth and eleventh grade. The program is one week long and the college pays all expenses, including travel. (See Summer for Free, page 92.) March 1 is the preferred date for nominations, the first step in the application process. **Clark University's Summer Science Program** is three weeks long and free for the taking for students who have completed eleventh grade. **CMU's Summer Programs for Diversity** are free, six-week programs for rising eleventh and twelfth graders in math, science, and fine arts.

Sunday, March 1

☐ Admission and financial aid deadlines at moderately selective private colleges and public universities

☐ Kaplan/*Newsweek* "My Turn" Essay Contest. www.kaptest.com/essay

☐ Clark University Summer Science Program Deadline. www.clarku.edu

☐ American Foreign Service High School Essay

Contest. www.afsa.org

☐ Pfizer Epilepsy Scholarship Award. www.epilepsy-scholarship.com

☐ Carnegie Mellon University—Summer Programs for Diversity. www.cmu.edu

☐ USDA 1890 National Scholarship. 1890scholars.program.usda.gov

Monday, March 2

_____

_____

Tuesday, March 3

_____

_____

Wednesday, March 4

_____

_____

Thursday, March 5

☐ Scholar Athlete Milk Mustache of the Year
(SAMMY) Award. www.bodybymilk.com

Friday, March 6

_____

_____

Saturday, March 7

_____

_____

How Counselors Use Their Connections

Parents may not say so out loud, but many expect more from a college counselor than simply sending off the transcripts and offering a good piece of advice now and then. They want a counselor who, when the chips are down, can pull the right string and get a kid into college.

Does it happen in real life? Maybe once in a while, but not in the way that most people envision. Here are some ways that high school counselors and admission officers typically interact:

- **They go over the list of applicants.** When a high school sends more than two or three applicants to a particular private college, the college counselor and admission officer often talk. The AO may call with a tentative list of decisions to get the counselor's feedback.

- **They discuss concerns.** Sometimes people on either side of the desk will want to talk about a concern related to a particular student, such as a blip in grades or a health issue. Uncertainty about an item on the transcript is another common topic.

- **The counselor may lobby for a particular student.** Counselors do make these calls, but smart ones do so only when they can meaningfully add to what has been submitted on paper. For instance, a student who contributes more to the intellectual life of the school than is reflected in his grades might be the subject of an "extra push" call by the counselor.

Counselors know that they cannot overplay their hand and make every candidate look like the greatest thing since sliced bread. Veteran counselors do have relationships with top admission officers, greased by annual conferences they both attend. Counselors at big-name private high schools or major suburban publics have a degree of clout at colleges where they send large numbers of students. Yet these same counselors could tell you a sad story about how the admit rate for traditional feeder high schools has steadily declined at big-name colleges in the last twenty years.

For their part, colleges are not going to allow a counselor to pull the wool over their eyes. For years, Princeton famously refused to interact with high school counselors beyond official communications. (Relations have thawed with a new dean in charge.) A good counselor can help students make their case, but students are the only ones who can get themselves in.

> Some of the best essays are on ordinary topics. The student does not have to build houses in Guatemala, climb Mt. Fiji, or kick the winning goal in a soccer championship.
>
> —Counselor's heads-up

SEARCHING FOR SCHOLARSHIPS: THE LOCAL ANGLE

This book includes a listing of the most prominent national scholarships. Something from that list may work out, though all national scholarship programs are very competitive. For obvious reasons, students have better odds at awards offered in their local community or state. A search on www.fastweb.com may locate some of these, but there is no substitute for working with the guidance office to find local awards. These may be offered by neighborhood associations, civic groups, churches, doctors, dentists, car dealerships, TV stations, and anyone else who wants to lend a hand to young people while getting a bit of publicity. In larger metropolitan areas, a local foundation may produce a scholarship directory that will list many of these awards. Deadlines are often in the spring.

WHAT HAS GOTTEN INTO YOU? PARENTS WANT TO KNOW

This phrase is commonly heard from the mouths of bewildered moms and dads in the spring of twelfth grade. Call it senioritis, pre-separation conflict, or the I'm-scared-to-leave-home blues. In its most acute form, it leads to knockdown battles over everything from homework to curfew.

What's happening here? Psychologists tell us that one way people deal with impending separation is to provoke conflict. Often, the intensity of the fighting is directly proportional to the strength of the bond between parent and child. Some students become more rebellious, others more withdrawn. Parents tend to react in the former case by asserting more control, and in the latter case by pushing harder to communicate. Neither is likely to work.

Parents should not be undone by an escalation of conflict as graduation approaches. It is part of the territory. Don't frantically try to fix things—or think that you only have a few months! Accept the fact that your relationship may not be fully back to normal until son or daughter goes away and gets some much-needed perspective. As always, parents need to keep an even keel. Maintain reasonable limits while cutting them a little more slack as they approach the time of leave-taking.

March 8–14, 2009

If you are currently enrolled in an AP course, you will probably be automatically registered to take the exam. The fee is about $84, with limited financial assistance available that may vary from school to school. Check with your school's AP coordinator. About 60 percent of the schools nationwide offer AP courses. If you would like to take an AP test but attend one of the 40 percent of schools that do not offer them, or if you are homeschooled, March 15 is the deadline for you to contact a school that does offer AP to make arrangements to take the tests. If considering this option, head to www.collegeboard.com for an overview of what each test covers, or buy a prep book from among the many available in bookstores. AP courses are generally a year long, so covering all the material will take some doing.

Sunday, March 8

Monday, March 9

Tuesday, March 10

Wednesday, March 11

_____   _____
_____   _____
_____   _____

Thursday, March 12

_____   _____
_____   _____
_____   _____

Friday, March 13

☐ April ACT late-registration deadline (approximate)   _____
_____   _____
_____   _____

Saturday, March 14

☐ SAT administered   _____
_____   _____
_____   _____

MARCH 15–21, 2009

The week's admission deadlines include **University of Minnesota at Morris** and **Wittenberg.** With spring break around the corner, now is the time for the Class of 2010 to follow through on making arrangements for any college visits.

The **Hispanic Scholarship Fund** sponsors a variety of awards with various corporate partners. Among the nation's most unique summer programs is the **Freeman Asian Cultural Experience** in Sewanee, which offers participants a free two-week program for students who have completed tenth or eleventh grade. (See Summer for Free, page 92.) Also in the summer, **Landmark Volunteers** offers dozens of community service programs throughout the nation. The program is available to students who have completed grades nine through eleven and costs $1,250 in the form of a tax-deductible contribution for a two-week experience. The **Ayn Rand Institute** offers awards of up to $2,000 to ninth and tenth graders for essays on Rand's novel *Anthem*.

Sunday, March 15

☐ Admission deadlines at moderately selective colleges

☐ AP Exam registration deadline for homeschooled students and those at schools not offering AP

☐ Hispanic Scholarship Fund deadline.
www.hispanicfund.org

☐ FACES Asian Studies Summer Program deadline.
www.sewanee.edu

☐ Landmark Volunteers deposit deadline.
www.volunteers.com

Monday, March 16

_____

_____

Tuesday, March 17

_____

_____

Wednesday, March 18

_____

_____

Thursday, March 19

_____

_____

Friday, March 20

☐ Ayn Rand Essay Contest.
www.aynrand.org/contests

_____

_____

Saturday, March 21

_____

_____

_____

_____

Taking a Year Off

> Regardless of why they took the year off or what they did, students could not be more effusive in their praise. Many talk of their year away as a "life-altering" experience or "turning point," and most feel that its full value can never be measured and will pay dividends the rest of their lives.
>
> —Harvard University website

Count Harvard among those who recommend—emphatically—that students consider taking a year off between high school and college. A prime candidate is the student who is weary of the rat race—who studies hard but has forgotten why. Students considering a year off before college should complete the admission process with everyone else. Then, after the offers of admission come back, the student should write a letter to the first-choice college asking for a deferral of enrollment for one year. Most colleges will be happy to grant such a request with a reasonable outline of what the student plans to do. Students can always change their minds and go to a different college after the year off, but they will have the peace of mind that comes with a reserved spot in a class.

There are some potential glitches. Sometimes scholarships cannot be postponed a year, including some state-sponsored scholarships that are open to high school graduates. Without a concrete plan, a year off can be counterproductive, especially if the student becomes passive or takes a menial job that does not further personal growth.

Students considering a year off may want to consult one of the following:

- *The Back Door Guide to Short-Term Job Adventures: Internships, Extraordinary Experiences, Seasonal Jobs, Volunteering, Work Abroad,* by Michael Landes (Ten Speed Press)

- *Taking Time Off,* by Colin Hall and Ron Lieber (Princeton Review)

LIVING/LEARNING AND RESIDENTIAL COLLEGE PROGRAMS

Many high school students are star-struck at the thought of rubbing shoulders with the multitudes at a sprawling university. So much to do, so many new faces. They don't count on the fact that anonymity can breed alienation, and that falling asleep in the back of a five-hundred-seat lecture hall is not the recipe for a quality education.

Some major universities have a great invention for dealing with this problem: a residential college or living/learning unit. Such programs offer the benefits of a small community while retaining access to the vast resources beyond. The living/learning component comes in the form of, say, a lecture in the residence hall common room, or a trip to the symphony for everyone in the program, or maybe a seminar offered only to students in the living/learning hall. A number of private universities, including Yale, U of Miami, and Rice, to name three, divide the whole student body into residential colleges. The most famous living/learning program among public institutions is the University of Michigan's one-thousand-student Residential College. Other public institutions with residential colleges include UC–San Diego, UC–Santa Cruz, University of Illinois at Urbana-Champaign, UMass, UNC–Chapel Hill, and University of Wisconsin at Madison, to name a representative sample.

Conventional honors programs at state universities provide similar benefits, including small classes, access to top faculty, and enrichment programming. Living/learning and honors programs are two great ways to get a private college education at a state university price.

> To really know what's going on at a college, talk to the maintenance staff and campus security. Go off the beaten path to look at buildings that were not included in the official tour.
>
> —Counselor's heads-up

MARCH 22–28, 2009

With spring break at hand, the Class of 2010 has a perfect chance for some serious thinking about summer. Students should focus less on what they think will "look good" than on what they really want to do. Summer programs at colleges cost a king's ransom but provide a great taste of college life. Deadlines are typically in April or May. Summer work is perfectly honorable. So, too, is a shadowing experience or internship in a field of potential interest.

Sunday, March 22

_____   _____

_____   _____

_____   _____

Monday, March 23

_____   _____

_____   _____

_____   _____

Tuesday, March 24

_____   _____

_____   _____

_____   _____

Wednesday, March 25

Thursday, March 26

Friday, March 27

Saturday, March 28

MARCH 29–31, 2009

For the Class of 2009, the **Young American Creative Patriotic Art** award features three one-time scholarships of $10,000 and is available to students in grades 9–12. One of the nation's biggest providers of scholarships for minority students, the **Jackie Robinson Foundation,** offers scholarships of up to $24,000 over four years for students who are American citizens.

Sunday, March 29

Monday, March 30

Tuesday, March 31

☐ May SAT and Subject Tests, registration deadline

☐ Young American Creative Patriotic Art Award.
www.ladiesauxvfw.com

☐ Jackie Robinson Foundation Scholarship.
www.jackierobinson.org

AN APPLICANT'S WORST NIGHTMARE: CAUGHT WITHOUT A SCHOOL

A denial from First Choice U is bad enough, but the worst-case scenario in college admission is getting a thin letter from every school on the list. Such cases are rare, but they are happening more frequently in today's competitive climate.

If, God forbid, you get caught in this situation, there are a number of paths to consider:

- **Try again at the same schools.** This strategy has the best chance of success for students who are on the waitlist. Your college counselor is probably best positioned to tell the sad story, which can increase the odds of admission if and when the waitlist becomes active. (See page 216 for more on the waitlist.)

- **Find new options.** Colleges don't like to say it too loudly, but plenty of them will consider strong applicants after April 1. A "spaces available" list circulates among high school counselors in late April, but even schools that are not on that list may find room. An acceptance can come within days.

- **Plan on a transfer.** A string of denials may indicate that the student's original college list was unrealistic. The student may choose to attend a community college or local state university with an eye toward transferring after a (one hopes) better academic performance next year.

- **Consider a postgraduate year.** Some boarding schools offer this option to students who have potential but need another year to mature. The environment tends to be structured and is no one's idea of fun, but students who do well may find their admission prospects drastically improved.

No one deserves the experience of having to scramble for a school in April. The good news is that for those who must do so, there are some reasonable options.

APRIL–JUNE 2009

SENIORS SHOULD WEIGH OFFERS, MAKE VISITS, and evaluate aid awards. Families can appeal low awards using a second, higher award as leverage. Waitlisted students should follow up promptly and vigorously. (See page 216.) Students wishing to take a year off before college should contact the colleges by phone and follow up with a letter. Students should reply to all offers of admission—including those they choose not to accept—by a postmark deadline of May 1.

The Class of 2010 should continue researching colleges with a goal of finding ten to twelve likely options by the end of school. Families should firm up summer plans and schedule college visits. Juniors applying to highly selective colleges should consider taking SAT Subject Tests in June.

WHAT TO DO:

✓ **Wednesday, April 1**
Decisions at the most selective colleges mailed and available on the Web

✓ **Saturday, April 4**
ACT administered

✓ **Saturday, May 2**
SAT and Subject Tests administered

✓ **Tuesday, May 5***
June SAT and Subject Tests registration deadline*

✓ **Friday, May 8**
June ACT registration deadline*

✓ **Saturday, June 6**
SAT and Subject Tests administered

✓ **Saturday, June 13**
ACT administered

*Approximate deadline. Check with www.collegeboard.com or www.act.org.

April 1–4, 2009

The nation's most selective colleges hand down their decisions on or about April 1. Drum roll, please. . . As a parent, you should stay calm and above the fray. Reassure your student, repeatedly if necessary, that any college selection will offer great opportunities. If he or she has applied intelligently, you'll be telling the truth.

The **Yoshiyama Award,** based solely on community service, requires a nomination and nets winners a one-time award of $5,000. Sponsored by the American Museum of Natural History, the **Young Naturalist Awards** offer up to $2,500 for outstanding projects in biology, earth science, and astronomy.

Wednesday, April 1

☐ Decisions at highly selective colleges mailed or available on the Web

☐ Yoshiyama Award. www.hitachi.org/yoshiyama

☐ Young Naturalist Awards. www.amnh.org

Thursday, April 2

Friday, April 3

_____   _____

_____   _____

_____   _____

Saturday, April 4

☐ ACT administered
                                   _____

_____   _____

_____   _____

THE NITTY GRITTY OF AID AWARDS

Only an accountant could enjoy the mind-numbing job of sifting through aid awards. The devil is in the details, so get out your magnifying glass. Your final decision probably won't depend on a thousand dollars here or there, but getting on top of the aid situation may help you pry more money from the college of choice. In the case of a toss-up, dollars may indeed make the difference. Here are some suggestions for evaluating aid awards:

- **Be systematic.** Need-based aid packages are a combination of grants (money you keep), loans (money you pay back), and work-study (the promise of government-subsidized employment to help pay the bills). The total amount of your aid package is less important than the amount of each component.

- **Check the cost assumptions.** If a college says it is meeting your full need, does it factor in an allowance for travel and living expenses? Some colleges consider these expenses in their awards; others do not, or do so with low-ball figures—which means the aid package won't cover the real bill.

- **Consider PLUS loans radioactive.** Some colleges don't meet the full financial need of applicants but want to look like they do. They pad their "aid" packages with market-rate PLUS loans that anyone can get, regardless of need. Look for loans that are "subsidized"—that means the government will pay the interest while the student is in school.

> I tried to make sure that my son had seen a variety of schools and understood what my opinion was and why it was my opinion. Then I let him choose.
>
> —University of Illinois at Urbana-Champaign dad

- **Find out about next year.** Is your merit scholarship renewable for four years? If so, the college should tell you the minimum GPA necessary to retain it. The usual is 3.0. Will the loan component of your package increase? The answer is probably yes—find out how much more in student loans will be expected during the upperclass years.

• **Use better need-based offers as leverage.** If the front-runner college doesn't come through with the top financial aid offer, send a copy of the best offer to its aid office, along with a tactful request to review the calculations. Be sure to highlight special circumstances that other colleges may have considered more generously.

A few institutions, notably Williams College and Carnegie Mellon University, openly say that they will match other need-based offers in some circumstances. Many colleges will make an upward adjustment if you give them a rationale. (Merit awards, on the other hand, are usually firm.) Parents often do the heavy lifting with a financial aid appeal, but they should encourage their kids to take the lead when the students are comfortable doing so. A student's best ally is the admission officer who did the recruiting—call and see if the AO can help in dealing with the financial aid office.

Though thousands of dollars may be at stake, the issue of how the college deals with your appeal may be as important as the dollars involved. An offer of admission and aid is the beginning of a four-year relationship. The way you are treated now may be a barometer of how you will be treated later.

> I found that whenever I visited a school during cold or bad weather, I had a less favorable impression of the school. My advice would be to try to block out influences like this.
>
> —Colby College student

DECISIONS, DECISIONS . . .

In the throes of making a final decision, some students almost wish they had been accepted at only one school. After months of hoping, waiting, and wondering, students must now choose one place to go and send the equivalent of a rejection letter to the others. Add guilt to the roller coaster of emotions. Here are some pointers for making a good choice:

> Students should visit, eat the food, attend a class, and experience the school before paying the cash.
>
> —Counselor's heads-up

- **Consider visiting again.** Our recommendation is strongest for students whose first visit was in the summer. For any student, it is amazing how different a campus can look with a freshly mailed acceptance letter in hand.

- **Focus on the fit rather than the admission officer.** Students can develop strong attachments to AOs during the course of the process. This is not necessarily a bad thing, unless a great recruiter sells you the wrong college.

- **Make lists, clarify priorities.** Students are in a different place at the end of the process than they were at the beginning. You should reexamine your priorities, and then compare and contrast the strengths of each choice based on those priorities.

- **Consult widely.** Students should compare notes with classmates, visit the guidance office, and call older friends who are already attending the colleges. They should even consider talking to Mom and Dad.

After all the analyzing—or even before—most students know in their hearts where they want to go. Parents should use the advice above to help them uncover the truth that is already inside them.

Some Acceptance Letters We'd Like to See (Translated for Parents)

With the euphoria of acceptance still fresh for students, the grim reality for parents may now be sinking in:

"Congratulations! You've earned a place in the Class of 2013."
Congratulations! Your child has earned the right to pay us $200,000 of your money.

"The college has reviewed your credentials and is confident of your potential for success."
The college has reviewed your net worth and will leave you just enough money to maintain the lifestyle of a hunter–gatherer.

"In the weeks ahead, you'll receive an official welcome to the college community."
. . . it will include an official envelope in which to enclose your check. Payment is due in July.

APRIL 5–JUNE 15, 2009

The final weeks of high school are a whirlwind. After chomping at the bit for months and years, students tend to be taken aback by how fast the end comes. Take time to savor the moment.

For many students, the last act of serious school will be AP exams during the second and third weeks of May. Waitlisted students will probably learn their fate by mid-May, though occasionally the uncertainty can drag on into the summer. Here are a few last deadlines.

Scholarships and Contests

Wednesday, April 15

☐ **AMVETS National Scholarship Deadline. (12) www.amvets.org**
The AMVETS scholarship offers six awards of $4,000 to veterans and their dependents.

☐ **Signet Classic Essay Contest.**
Five scholarships of $1,000 each for students in grades 11–12 who write a 2–3 page essay.

Monday, April 20

☐ **Society of Hispanic Engineers Scholarship. (12) www.shpe.org**
Scholarships of up to $3000 via a variety of programs.

Saturday, April 25

☐ **The Ayn Rand Essay Contest.**
(12) www.aynrand.org/contests
Sponsored by the foundation that carries on the work of the famed novelist/philosopher, this contest offers sixteen one-time awards between $1,000 and $10,000 for essays on *The Fountainhead*.

Thursday, April 30

☐ **Holocaust Remembrance Essay Contest. (9–12)**
www.holocaust.hklaw.com
The Holocaust Remembrance Essay Contest makes ten one-time awards of $10,000, along with smaller cash prizes.

Friday, May 1

☐ **Jane Austen Society Essay Contest. (9–12) www.jasna.org**
The Jane Austen Society offers a one-time prize of $1,000 for first place in its essay contest.

Friday, May 8

☐ **American Fire Sprinkler Association Essay Contest. (12) www.afsascholarship.org**
Less obscure than you might think, this contest offers a shot at one of ten scholarships of $2,000.

Friday, May 15

☐ **Society of Women Engineers Scholarship. (12) www.swe.org**
The Society of Women Engineers offers about twenty-five renewable scholarships of up to $5,000 per year to future engineers, male as well as female.

Monday, June 1

☐ **Arts Recognition and Talent Search, Early Deadline. (11) www.nfaa.org**
The National Foundation for the Advancement of the Arts sponsors the Arts Recognition and Talent Search (ARTS), one of the nation's most prestigious competitions for students in dance, film and video, jazz, music, photography, theater, visual arts, voice, and writing. Hundreds of one-time scholarships of up to $25,000 are available. The program is also the gateway to the Presidential Scholars in the Arts recognition program. June 1 is an early deadline with a second round on October 1.

☐ **Donna Reed Performing Arts Scholarships. (12) www.donnareed.org**
These scholarships include ten awards of $1,000 for students who excel in acting and musical theater.

Monday, June 15

☐ **SAR Rumbaugh Oration Contest (12) www.sar.org**
The Sons of the American Revolution sponsor this oration contest, open to students in grades 10–12, which requires a 5–6 minute oration for scholarships of up to $3,000.

STANDARDIZED TESTING APRIL–JUNE 2009

Thursday, April 9
May SAT and Subject Tests late-registration deadline (approximate)

Saturday, May 2
SAT and Subject Tests administered

Tuesday, May 5
June SAT and Subject Tests registration deadline (approximate)

Friday, May 8
June ACT registration deadline

Thursday, May 14
June SAT and Subject Tests late-registration deadline (approximate)

Friday, May 22
June ACT late-registration deadline

Saturday, June 6
SAT and Subject Tests administered

Saturday, June 13
ACT administered

COPING WITH THE WAITLIST

The college application process is stressful enough when the answers come back as either a yes or a no. Nothing is more agonizing than getting a maybe— as in, "You've waited four months for our decision and you are really close to getting in, so please stay on our waitlist for another month or two."

Colleges use the waitlist because they are not sure how many of the accepted applicants will actually enroll. The waitlist is their margin of safety to ensure that the class is full. The odds of acceptance from the waitlist are generally less than 50/50, but may vary depending on the college and the year. Waitlists are seldom ranked.

Waitlisted students should think hard about whether pursuing admission will be worth the time, effort, and agony. Though most students learn their fate by the end of May, some are left dangling into the summer.

Before doing anything, waitlisted students must send a deposit and communicate their intent to enroll at another institution that did offer an acceptance. There is no need to tell the accepting college about the other college's waitlist.

> Set aside time for writing essays and filling out applications. I almost didn't finish my essays before the application deadline because I got bogged down with schoolwork and extracurricular activities.
>
> —Vanderbilt University student

For the waitlist, most colleges ask that students return a postcard indicating interest. But that's only the beginning. The waitlist is an all-or-nothing proposition that should include one or more of the following, done by mid-April:

- A letter to the admission director communicating an unquenchable desire to attend the college. Strong letters include thoughtful discussion about why the fit is right and updates on any new honors or achievements.

- A campus interview, especially if you have not already had one. Nothing beats a chance to make the case face to face.

- Another recommendation from a current teacher highlighting your achievements in twelfth grade, or a sample of your recent best work.

- A phone call from your college counselor, highlighting the fact that your third-quarter grades are good (they better be) and reinforcing your willingness to attend if accepted.

Unfortunately, many colleges do not have much or any financial aid for waitlisted students. Full-payers are the most likely to get in off the waitlist, and those who applied for aid should emphasize their willingness to attend with or without aid if they can realistically do so.

Colleges use spots on the waitlist to make dreams come true for a lucky handful who go all-out for admission.

For Parents: The Summer before Leaving

With crying towels at the ready, we offer a few thoughts for Mom and Dad. Most important, be prepared for the continuation of the aloof/emotional/standoffish behavior that may have marked the senior year. Fear of leaving is acted out in strange ways and is not a commentary on your relationship with your son or daughter. Roll with the punches and keep both feet on the ground. As the summer wanes, expect your child to spend every possible moment with friends. They'll miss you too, but don't count on seeing any evidence of that fact. Here are some things to do as the clock winds down.

Loosen the Reigns

We're not suggesting that you compromise major principles or let them run wild. Just ease up a bit. They'll be on their own in a month or two anyway.

> Practice your interview with a counselor, teacher, or friend. A firm handshake, clearly articulated speaking, and eye contact go a long way in making a great first impression.
>
> —Counselor's heads-up

They can spend their last few weeks fighting with you over curfew, or they can begin to adjust to the freedom they will have on campus.

Suggest a Packing List

Mom should fight the temptation to make one. Instead, suggest that your child talk to friends or older peers for ideas about what to bring. Make sure the college has informed you specifically about the dorms and what it thinks your son or daughter will need. Consult with the college before buying a computer.

Discuss Finances

College students are bombarded with credit card applications from the moment they set foot on campus. Now is the time to impart a little financial savvy. What are their prerogatives related to credit cards? Will they open a checking account? How much spending money will they get? All these things should be discussed in advance.

Have Them Attend Orientation

Colleges often have a variety of orientation programs, from a standard campus introduction to weeklong adventure trips. Encourage your son or daughter to do one. A few good friends made at such programs can be a comfort during the initial days of the semester.

> My best interview was less like an interview and more like a conversation.
>
> —Reed College student

Don't Linger When You Drop Them Off

During the first days of college, parents have a status roughly equal to the lepers in Biblical times. We suggest that parents help the student settle in, make sure everything is OK, and then get a move on. When students are insecure about their identity in a new place, the last thing they want is to be seen with Mom and Dad.

Write Letters and Send Email

Every parent wants to keep in touch, but phone calls can be embarrassing when the new student is sitting in a room full of friends. Parents should start out with letters and email and encourage the

student to make the first phone call. College students really do want to hear from parents (even if they won't admit it).

Have Realistic Expectations

The first year of college is an emotional roller coaster and far from the carefree time that many of us think we remember. Students should be prepared for some rocky times along with the excitement, and parents should expect at least one or two teary phone calls. Only if the unhappiness persists for a period of months should anyone become concerned.

A final suggestion for parents after they drop off their son or daughter: Do something nice for yourself. Go on a cruise or visit a place you've always wanted to go. Your child will be fine, and you've got a life to live, too.

> Never send in your application without asking someone else to proofread it.
>
> —Counselor's heads-up

A NOTE ON THE APPENDICES

The pages that follow include key deadlines and requirements at the nation's three hundred "best and most interesting" colleges, as selected by the *Fiske Guide to Colleges*, where students will find a comprehensive write-up on each.

Appendix A: Standardized Tests
SAT and Subject Tests Calendar—2008–2009
ACT Assessment Calendar 2008–2009
Colleges That Require SAT Subject Tests for Admission
Colleges That Recommend SAT Subject Tests

Appendix B: Admission Deadlines
Early-Decision Deadlines
Early-Action Deadlines
Regular Admission Deadlines

Appendix C: Scholarship Deadlines
Independent Scholarships and Awards
General Interest Scholarships and Awards
Minority Interest Scholarships and Awards
Science and Technology-Related Scholarships and Awards
Essay Contests
Early-Bird Institutional Scholarships

APPENDIX A: STANDARDIZED TESTS

SAT AND SUBJECT TESTS CALENDAR — SPRING 2008

Test Date	Test Offered	Registration Deadline	Late Registration
January 26, 2008	SAT & Subject Tests	December 26, 2007	January 4, 2008
March 1, 2008	SAT only	January 29, 2008	February 7, 2008
May 3, 2008	SAT & Subject Tests	April 1, 2008	April 10, 2008
June 7, 2008	SAT & Subject Tests	May 6, 2008	May 15, 2008

SAT AND SUBJECT TESTS CALENDAR — 2008–2009

Test Date	Test Offered	Approximate Registration Deadline	Approximate Late Registration
October 4, 2008	SAT & Subject Tests	September 8, 2008	September 12, 2008
November 1, 2008	SAT & Subject Tests	September 30, 2008	October 9, 2008
December 6, 2008	SAT & Subject Tests	October 4, 2008	November 13, 2008
January 24, 2009	SAT & Subject Tests	December 24, 2008	January 2, 2009
March 1, 2009	SAT only	January 25, 2009	February 8, 2009
May 2, 2009	SAT & Subject Tests	March 31, 2009	April 9, 2009
June 6, 2009	SAT & Subject Tests	May 5, 2009	May 14, 2009

At press time, the College Board had not released the registration and late-registration deadlines for 2008–2009. The dates above are projections based on past years. Visit www.collegeboard.com to confirm these dates.

All dates are postmark deadlines for students in the United States. (Receipt dates for those outside the U.S.) Students can also register at www.collegeboard.com. For students who cannot test on Saturday for religious reasons, the tests will be offered on the Sunday immediately following. March and April test dates are available only in the U.S.

ACT Assessment Calendar—Spring 2008

Test Date	Registration Deadline	Late Registration
February 9, 2008**	January 4, 2008	January 18, 2008
April 12, 2008	March 7, 2008	March 21, 2008
June 14, 2008	May 9, 2008	May 23, 2008

** Not available in the state of New York.
All dates are postmark deadlines.

ACT Assessment Calendar—2008–2009

Test Date	Approximate Registration Deadline	Approximate Late Registration
September 13, 2008*	August 13, 2008	August 22, 2008
October 25, 2008	September 19, 2008	October 3, 2008
December 13, 2008	November 7, 2008	November 20, 2008
February 7, 2009**	January 2, 2009	January 16, 2009
April 4, 2009	February 27, 2009	March 13, 2009
June 13, 2009	May 8, 2009	May 22, 2009

*Available only in Arizona, California, Florida, Georgia, Illinois, Indiana, Maryland, Nevada, North Carolina, Pennsylvania, South Carolina, Texas, and Washington.

**Not available in the state of New York.
All dates are postmark deadlines. At press time, ACT had not released the registration and late-registration deadlines for 2008–2009. The dates above are projections based on past years. Visit www.act.org to confirm these dates.

COLLEGES THAT REQUIRE SAT SUBJECT TESTS FOR ADMISSION

Institutions requiring Subject Tests are confined to the East Coast and California. The colleges below require either two or three tests, as noted below. Some colleges allow students to choose any test; others stipulate particular ones. Many colleges allow students to submit an ACT score instead of one or more Subject Test scores.

Amherst College (2)
Barnard College (2)
Boston College (2)
Boston University (2)
Brandeis University (2)
Brown University (2)
Bryn Mawr College (2)
University of California (all campuses) (2)
California Institute of Technology (2)
Carnegie Mellon University (2)
Catholic University (placement only)
Columbia University (2)
Connecticut College (2)
Cooper Union (engineering only) (2)
Cornell University (2)
Dartmouth College (2)
Duke University (2)
Georgetown University (3)
Harvard University (3)

Harvey Mudd College (2)
Haverford College (2)
Massachusetts Institute of Technology (3)
McGill University (2)
Northwestern University Integrated Science Program (3)
    and Honors Program in Medical Education (2)
University of Pennsylvania (2)
Pomona College (2)
Princeton University (3)
Rice University (2)
Swarthmore College (2)
Vassar College (2)
University of Virginia (2)
Washington & Lee University (2)
Wellesley College (2)
Wesleyan University (2)
Williams College (2)
Yale University (2)

COLLEGES THAT RECOMMEND SAT SUBJECT TESTS

Students who are required to take Subject Tests by other institutions should forward their scores to these colleges. Students not otherwise planning to take Subject Tests should consult with these colleges as to whether they should take the tests. Some colleges ask for Subject scores only for placement. Students who are taking the ACT may be able to submit scores from it in lieu of taking the Subject Tests.

American University
Babson College
Carleton College
Case Western Reserve University
Davidson College
Emory University
University of Georgia
George Washington
Hamilton College
Johns Hopkins University
Lafayette College
Lehigh University
Mary Washington College
Mills College
New York University
University of North Carolina at Chapel Hill
Northwestern University

Oberlin College
Occidental College
Reed College
University of Rochester
Skidmore College
Smith College
University of Southern California
Southern Methodist University (some programs)
Stanford University
Stevens Institute of Technology
Sweet Briar College
University of Texas at Austin
Wake Forest University
Washington University in St. Louis
Wheaton College (IL)
Whitman College
College of William & Mary

Appendix B: Admission Deadlines

Early-Decision Deadlines

ED applicants are obligated to attend the college if accepted. Students may apply to only one college via early decision and must withdraw all other applications if accepted. Some colleges have two early-decision deadlines. In such cases, the second ED deadline is denoted with a (II).

October 31
California Polytechnic State University/San Luis Obispo

November 1
Boston University
Brown University
Carnegie Mellon University
Columbia University
Cornell College (IA)
Cornell University (NY)
Dartmouth College
DePauw University
Duke University
Elon University
Emory University
Ithaca College
Johns Hopkins University
Middlebury College
Miami University (OH)
University of Miami (FL)
New York University
Northwestern University
University of Pennsylvania
Pomona College

Rensselaer Polytechnic Institute
Rhodes College
Rice University
St. Olaf College
Scripps College
Southwestern University
Spelman College
Stetson University
Trinity University (TX)
Tufts University
Tulane University
Vanderbilt University
Virginia Tech
Wellesley College
College of William and Mary
Wheaton College (MA)

November 10
Williams College
George Washington University
University of North Carolina–Asheville

November 15
Agnes Scott College

Allegheny College
American University
Amherst College
Babson College
Barnard College
Bates College
Bennington College
Bowdoin College
Brandeis University
Bryn Mawr College
Bucknell University
Carleton College
Carnegie Mellon University
Claremont McKenna College
Clark University
Colby College
Colgate University
College of New Jersey
Colorado College
Connecticut College
Davidson College
Dickinson College
Eugene Lang College
Franklin & Marshall College
Furman University
Gettysburg College
Gordon College
Hamilton College
Hampden-Sydney College
Hampshire College
Hartwick College
Harvey Mudd College
Haverford College
Hobart and William Smith Colleges
Kalamazoo College

Kenyon College
Lawrence University
Lehigh University
Marlboro College
Morehouse College
Mount Holyoke College
College of New Jersey
Oberlin College
Occidental College
Pitzer College
University of Puget Sound
Randolph College
Reed College
University of Richmond
University of Rochester
Rollins College
St. Lawrence University
Sarah Lawrence College
Skidmore College
Smith College
University of the South (Sewanee)
State University of New York–Geneseo
Stevens Institute of Technology
Susquehanna University
Swarthmore College
Syracuse University
Trinity College (CT)
Union College
Vassar College
Wabash College
Wake Forest University
Warren Wilson College
Washington University in St. Louis
Washington & Lee University
Wesleyan University

Whitman College
Wittenberg University
Wofford College

November 20
Grinnell College

November 30
Cooper Union (engineering only)

December 1
Alfred University
College of the Atlantic
Carnegie Mellon University (II)
Clarkson University
Denison University
Drew University
Earlham College
Hollins University
Lake Forest College
Manhattanville College
Marlboro College
Ohio Wesleyan University
Rochester Institute of Technology
St. Mary's College of Maryland
Sweet Briar College
Washington & Jefferson College
College of Wooster

December 3
Cooper Union (art only)

December 15
College of the Holy Cross
University of Puget Sound (II)
Wells College

December 28
Pomona College (II)

January 1
Bates College (II)
Bennington College (II)
Boston University (II)
Bowdoin College (II)
Brandeis University (II)
Bryn Mawr College (II)
Bucknell University (II)
Claremont McKenna College (II)
Colby College (II)
Colorado College (II)
Connecticut College (II)
Davidson College (II)
Emory University (II)
Grinnell College (II)
Hamilton College (II)
Hobart and William Smith Colleges (II)
Lafayette College
Lehigh University (II)
Macalester College (II)
Middlebury College (II)
Mount Holyoke College (II)
Oberlin College (II)

Reed College (II)
Rhodes College (II)
Sarah Lawrence College (II)
Scripps College (II)
Smith College (II)
University of the South (Sewanee) (II)
Southwestern University (II)
Susquehanna University (II)
Swarthmore College (II)
Trinity College (CT) (II)
Tufts University (II)
Vanderbilt University (II)
Vassar College (II)
Washington & Lee University (II)
Wesleyan University (II)
Whitman College (II)

January 10
College of the Atlantic (II)
George Washington University (II)

January 15
Carleton College (II)

Colgate University (II)
Dickinson College (II)
Drew University (II)
Franklin & Marshall College (II)
Gettysburg College (II)
Hartwick College (II)
Kenyon College (II)
University of Richmond (II)
University of Rochester (II)
St. Lawrence University (II)
St. Mary's College of Maryland (II)
Skidmore College (II)
Stevens Institute of Technology (II)
Union College (II)
Ursinus College
Wheaton College (MA) (II)
College of Wooster (II)

February 1
Muhlenberg College

Applying EA does not obligate students to attend if accepted. Students may weigh other offers until the May 1 reply date. Some colleges have two early-action deadlines. In such cases, the second EA deadline is denoted with a (II).

A few universities with EA programs, notably Yale and Stanford, forbid students who apply EA from applying early to another institution. This program, known as "single choice early action," is relatively new. Check with the college if you are in doubt as to whether you retain the right to apply early at another institution. All deadlines are current as of press time, but we strongly suggest that applicants verify them with the colleges.

October 1
University of South Carolina

October 15
University of Georgia

October 31
University of Michigan

November 1
Alma College
Auburn University
Bard College
Boston College
California Institute of Technology
Case Western Reserve University
University of Dallas
University of Denver
Fordham University
Georgetown University
Howard University
James Madison University
Lewis and Clark College
University of Massachusetts at Amherst
Massachusetts Institute of Technology
University of Miami (FL)
University of North Carolina at Chapel Hill

North Carolina State University
University of Notre Dame
Santa Clara University
Southern Methodist University
Stanford University
University of Tennessee
Trinity University (TX)
Tulane University
University of Vermont
Villanova University
Wheaton College (IL)
Willamette University
Yale University

November 10
Elon University
University of North Carolina at Asheville

November 15
Albertson College
University of Arkansas
Babson College
Catholic University
University of Chicago
Colorado College
DePaul University
Fairfield University
Illinois Institute of Technology (architecture only)

Mills College
Northeastern University
University of the Pacific
Pepperdine University
Presbyterian College
University of San Francisco
Spelman College
State University of New York at Albany
State University of New York at Binghamton
Texas Christian University
Truman State University
Worcester Polytechnic Institute

December 1

Albion College
Austin College
Beloit College
Butler University
Centre College
University of Connecticut
Cornell College (IA)
University of Dallas (II)
Depauw University
Dickinson College
Drexel University
Gordon College
Goucher College
Hampshire College
Hood College (II)
Kalamazoo College
Knox College
Lake Forest College
Lawrence University
University of Maryland
University of New Hampshire
Rice University
Rollins College

St. John's University (MN)
St. Olaf College
Simmons College
Ursinus College
Whittier College
Willamette University (II)
Wittenberg University

December 5

Oglethorpe University
Presbyterian College (II)

December 15

University of Maine
Ohio Wesleyan University
University of Rhode Island
Rhode Island School of Design
Trinity University (TX) (II)
Wabash College
Wells College

January 1

Earlham College
Wellesley College
Worcester Polytechnic Institute (II)

January 8

Millsaps College

January 15

Austin College (II)
Guilford College
Hampden-Sydney College
Illinois Institute of Technology (II) (architecture only)
Kalamazoo College (II)
University of Mary Washington
Washington and Jefferson College

November 1
University of Florida (priority)

November 10
University of Illinois at Urbana-Champaign (priority)

November 15
Deep Springs College

November 30
University of California (all campuses)
Pennsylvania State University (priority)

December 1
Carnegie Mellon University (fine arts only)
The Juilliard School
Marquette University (priority)
Rutgers—The State University of New Jersey (priority)
University of South Carolina (priority)
University of Washington (priority)

December 15
University of Minnesota (priority)

December 31
University of Notre Dame
Yale University

January 1
Amherst College

Barnard College
Bates College
Boston College
Boston University
Bowdoin College
Brown University
Bucknell University
Carnegie Mellon University
Colby College
Connecticut College
Cornell University
Dartmouth College
University of Dayton (priority)
Hamilton College
Harvard University
Johns Hopkins University
Lafayette College
Lehigh University
Massachusetts Institute of Technology
Middlebury College
Northwestern University
University of Pennsylvania
Pitzer College
Princeton University
University of Rochester
Sarah Lawrence College
Scripps College
Stanford University
Syracuse University
Trinity College (CT)
Tufts University
Vassar College

Wesleyan University
College of William & Mary
Williams College

January 2
California Institute of Technology
University of Chicago
Claremont McKenna College
Columbia University
Davidson College
Duke University
University of Illinois at Urbana-Champaign
Pomona College
Rice University
Swarthmore College
University of Virginia

January 3
Bennington College
Vanderbilt University

January 4
Cooper Union (architecture only)

January 5
Emerson College

January 7
Villanova University
Santa Clara University

January 10
Elon University

George Washington University
Georgetown University
Occidental College
University of Southern California

January 11
Cooper Union (art only)

January 15
American University
Babson College
Bard College
Beloit College
Brandeis University
Bryn Mawr College
Carleton College
Case Western Reserve University
University of Cincinnati
Clark University
Clarkson University
Colgate University
Colorado College
University of Colorado at Boulder
University of Delaware
Denison University
University of Denver
Emory University
Fairfield University
Fordham University
Furman University
University of Georgia
Georgia Institute of Technology
Hampshire College
Harvey Mudd College

Regular Admission Deadlines, continued

Haverford College
College of the Holy Cross
James Madison University
Kenyon College
Lawrence University
Macalester College
University of Massachusetts at Amherst
McGill University
Mount Holyoke College
State University of New York at Geneseo
New York University
Northeastern University
University of North Carolina at Chapel Hill
Oberlin College
University of the Pacific
Pepperdine University
Reed College
Rensselaer Polytechnic Institute
Rhodes College
University of Richmond
St. Mary's College of Maryland
St. Olaf College
Skidmore College
Smith College
Southern Methodist University
State University of New York at Binghamton
Tulane University
Union College
University of Vermont
Virginia Tech
Wake Forest University
University of Washington (WA)

Washington & Lee University
Washington University in St. Louis
Wellesley College
Wheaton College (IL)
Wheaton College (MA)
Whitman College

January 20
Grinnell College
University of Maryland

January 31
Miami University (OH)

February 1
Alfred University
University of Arkansas (priority)
Brigham Young University
Butler University
Centre College
Cooper Union (engineering only)
University of Connecticut
DePaul University
DePauw University
Dickinson College
Eugene Lang College
Franklin & Marshall College
George Mason University
Goucher College
Guilford College
University of Hawaii at Manoa (priority)

Hobart and William Smith Colleges
Hood College
Indiana University
Ithaca College
Knox College
Lewis and Clark College
University of Mary Washington
University of Miami (FL)
University of Michigan
University of New Hampshire
North Carolina State University (priority)
Ohio University
Oregon State University
Presbyterian College
University of Puget Sound
University of Rhode Island
Rochester Institute of Technology
St. Lawrence University
University of San Francisco
Simmons College
University of the South (Sewanee)
State University of New York—Geneseo
Sweet Briar College
University of Tennessee
Texas A&M University
University of Texas at Austin
Trinity University (TX)
Wabash College
Whittier College
Willamette University
University of Wisconsin at Madison
Wofford College
Worcester Polytechnic Institute

February 13
Florida State University

February 15
Albertson College (priority)
Allegheny College
College of the Atlantic
Catholic University
Drew University
Earlham College
Gettysburg College
Hartwick College
Hollins University (priority)
Howard University
Kalamazoo College
University of Kentucky
Lake Forest College
Marlboro College
Morehouse College
Muhlenberg College
New College of Florida (priority)
College of New Jersey
Rhode Island School of Design
Rollins College
Spelman College
Southwestern University
Stevens Institute of Technology
Texas Christian University
Ursinus College
College of Wooster

Regular Admission Deadlines, continued

February 16
University of North Carolina at Asheville

February 28
University of British Columbia
Warren Wilson College

March 1
Agnes Scott College
Albion College
Cornell College (IA)
University of Dallas
Drexel University
Evergreen State College
Gordon College
Hampden-Sydney College
Manhattanville College
Mills College
University of North Carolina at Greensboro
Ohio Wesleyan University
Purdue University
Randolph College
Rose-Hulman Institute of Technology
State University of New York at Albany
Stetson University
Susquehanna University
University of Toronto
Truman State University
Washington & Jefferson College
Wells College
West Virginia University

March 15
University of Minnesota at Morris
Wittenberg University

April 1
College of Charleston
University of Iowa
University of Kansas
University of Oklahoma
University of Utah

May 1
University of Arizona
Clemson University
Colorado School of Mines
University of Hawaii at Manoa
Texas Tech University

June 1
Albertson College
Albion College

Appendix C: Scholarship Deadlines

Independent Scholarships and Awards

These awards come from non-college sources and can therefore be used to cover costs at any institution in the country. All such awards mentioned in this book are listed here. We divide them into five categories: General Interest, Minority Interest, Science and Technology-Related Scholarships, Essay Contests, and Early-Bird Institutional Scholarships. Each list is in chronological order by deadline. Dates are for 2008 and may vary in succeeding years. Since deadlines are subject to change, we strongly recommend that you consult the websites referenced below for the latest information. For an overview of each award, consult the description of the appropriate week in the calendar.

This book lists many of the nation's most prestigious scholarships and prizes, but it does not provide a comprehensive list of all independent scholarships. For further information on the scholarship search, see the *Fiske Guide to Getting into the Right College,* 3E.

General Interest Scholarships and Awards

January 11
Sam Walton Community Scholarship.
   www.walmartfoundation.org
Elks Most Valuable Student Scholarship.
   www.elks.org/enf/scholars/mvs.cfm

January 18
National Honor Society Scholarship.
   www.nassp.org

January 31
Navy ROTC Scholarship. www.todaysmilitary.com
Discover Card Tribute Award.
   www.discovercard.com/tribute.htm

February 1
Junior Achievement Scholarship. www.ja.org
DAR Scholarships. www.dar.org
Phi Delta Kappa International Scholarship.
   www.pdkintl.org/studser/sschol.htm

February 6
American Foreign Service Association Scholarship.
   www.afsa.org

February 11
NFIB Young Entrepreneur Awards
   www.nfib.com

General Interest Scholarships and Awards, continued

February 20
USA Today All-USA High School Academic Team.
www.usatoday.com

March 1
Pfizer Epilepsy Scholarship. www.epilepsy-scholarship.com

March 5
Scholar Athlete Milk Mustache of the Year (SAMMY)
Award. www.whymilk.com

March 15
Horace Mann Student Scholarship Program.
www.horacemann.com

March 31
Young American Creative Patriotic Art Award.
www.ladiesauxvfw.com

April 1
Yoshiyama Award. www.hitachi.org/yoshiyama

April 15
AMVETS National Scholarship. www.amvets.org

June 1
NFAA Arts Recognition and Talent Search (ARTS), Early
Deadline. www.artsawards.org
Donna Reed Performing Arts Scholarships.
www.donnareed.org

June 15
Sons of the American Revolution Rumbaugh Oration
Contest. www.sar.org

September 30
The Tylenol Scholarship. www.scholarship.tylenol.com

October 1
NFAA Arts Recognition and Talent Search (ARTS), final
deadline. www.artsawards.org

October 10
Outstanding Students of America Scholarship.
www.outstandingstudentsofamerica.com

October 30
Horatio Alger Scholarship Program. www.horatioalger.com

October 31
Coca-Cola Scholars deadline. www.coca-colascholars.org
Prudential Spirit of Community Awards deadline.
www.prudential.com

November 1
VFW Voice of Democracy Scholarship.
www.vfw.org/yourtown/you_VoiceOf.htm
Susan G. Komen Breast Cancer Foundation College
Scholarship. www.komen.org/grants

November 15

Army ROTC Scholarship. www.armyrotc.com

November 30

National Security Agency, Undergraduate Training Program. www.nsa.gov

Defense Intelligence Agency Undergraduate Training Assistance Program. www.dia.mil

December 1

Toyota Community Scholars. www.toyota.com

Air Force ROTC Scholarship. www.afrotc.com

NASSP Principal's Leadership Award. www.principals.org

December 10

National Beta Club Scholarship. www.betaclub.org

National Academy of Television Arts and Sciences Scholarship. www.emmyonline.org/emmy/scholr.html

December 15

AXA Achievement Scholarship. www.axa-achievement.com

Burger King Scholars Program. www.burgerking.com

Deadline Varies

Scholastic Art and Writing Awards. www.scholastic.com/artandwritingawards

National History Day. www.nationalhistoryday.org

Junior Science and Humanities Symposium. www.jshs.org

U.S. Senate Youth Scholarship. (11–12). www.isbe.net/hearst

MINORITY INTEREST SCHOLARSHIPS AND AWARDS

January 9

Ron Brown Scholar Program. African Americans. www.ronbrown.org

January 11

Gates Millennium Scholarship. www.gmsp.org

February 15

U.S.A. Funds Access to Education Scholarship. www.usafunds.org

March 15

Hispanic Scholarship Fund, general deadline. www.hispanicfund.org

March 31

Jackie Robinson Foundation Scholarship. www.jackierobinson.org

April 20

Society of Hispanic Professional Engineers Scholarship. www.shpe.org

June 15

Hispanic Scholarship Fund/Society of Hispanic Professional Engineers Scholarship Program. www.shpe.org/scholarship

October 1

Hispanic Scholarship Fund/Toyota Scholarship Program. www.hsf.net/scholarship/seniors.php

December 15

Hispanic Scholarship Fund High School Scholarship. www.hsf.net/scholarships.php

SCIENCE AND TECHNOLOGY-RELATED SCHOLARSHIPS AND AWARDS

January 30
Toshiba/NSTA ExploraVision Awards.
www.exploravision.org

March 1
USDA 1890 National Scholars Program.
www.1890scholars.program.usda.gov

April 1
Young Naturalist Awards.
www.amnh.org

May 15
Society of Women Engineers Scholarship. www.swe.org

June 15
Hispanic Scholarship Fund/Society of Hispanic Professional
Engineers Scholarship Program. www.shpe.org/scholarship

October 1
Hispanic Scholarship Fund/Toyota Scholarship Program.
www.hsf.net/scholarship/seniors.php

October 2
Siemens Westinghouse Competition in Math, Science, and
Technology. www.siemens-foundation.org

November 15
Intel Science Talent Search. www.sciserv.org/isef

December 1
SAE Engineering Scholarship. www.sae.org

Deadline Varies
Intel Science and Engineering Fairs. www.sciserv.org/isef

Essay Contests

January 2
United Nations Association National High School Essay Contest. www.unausa.org

January 12
JFK Profile in Courage Essay Contest. www.jfkcontest.org

January 25
The DuPont Challenge Science Essay Contest. www.glcomm.com/dupont

February 1
U.S. Institute of Peace National Peace Essay Contest. www.usip.org/ed/npec/index.html

February 27
Optimist International Essay Contest. www.optimist.org

March 1
Kaplan/*Newsweek* "My Turn" Essay Contest. www.kaptest.com/essay
American Foreign Service Essay Contest. www.afsa.org

March 20
Ayn Rand Essay Contest (grades 9 and 10). www.aynrand.org/contests

April 1
Young Naturalist Awards. www.amnh.org/nationalcenter/youngnaturalistawards

April 16
Signet Classic Essay Contest. www.penguingroup.com

April 25
Ayn Rand Essay Contest (grades 11 and 12). www.aynrand.org/contests

April 30
Holocaust Remembrance Project Essay Contest. www.holocaust.hklaw.com

May 1
Jane Austen Society Essay Contest. www.jasna.org

May 9
American Fire Sprinkler Association Essay Contest. www.afsascholarship.org

June 1
Chemagination Essay Contest. www.chemistry.org

December 31
Sons of American Revolution Knight Essay Contest. www.sar.org
Mensa MERF Essay Contest. www.merf.us.mensa.org/scholarships/index.php

Early-Bird Institutional Scholarships

Institutional scholarships are sponsored by a college or university rather than an independent group. Since you can't take them anywhere aside from the institution that offers them, such scholarships tend to be easier to win than independent ones. And they also tend to be more lucrative. Unless otherwise noted, the scholarships in this list are renewable for four years, unlike most independent scholarships, which are one-time deals.

Many institutional scholarships are available to any applicant who applies for admission. But some awards require an early application. The following list includes institutional scholarships with a deadline before January 1—the kind that so often sneak up on unsuspecting applicants. Since deadlines are subject to change, we strongly recommend that you consult the colleges below for the latest information.

Some of the entries below are for a particular scholarship program. Others are general scholarship deadlines, meaning that some or all of the institution's scholarships are available only—or on a priority basis—to students who apply by the deadline noted. When grades and test scores are cited, such figures are the minimums for consideration.

October 5
University of North Carolina at Chapel Hill. Morehead-Cain Scholarship Nomination Deadline (participating schools only). Criteria: all-around excellence. Amount: full costs of attendance and summer stipend. ww.moreheadfoundation.org

October 15
Whittier College. Honors Weekend application deadline. Criteria: 3.5 GPA and 1200 SAT or 27 ACT. Amount: up to full tuition. www.whittier.edu

October 31
Georgia Institute of Technology. Presidential Scholarship. Criteria: academic excellence and leadership. Amount: up to the full costs of attendance. www.gatech.edu

November 1
Boston College. Presidential Scholars. Criteria: academic excellence, leadership, community service. Amount: scholarships up to full tuition. www.bc.edu

Emory University. Emory Scholars. Criteria: all-around excellence. Amount: up to full costs of attendance. School nomination required. www.emory.edu

Howard University. General scholarship deadline. Criteria: varies. Amount: up to the full costs of attendance. www.howard.edu

Indiana University. General scholarship priority deadline. Criteria: varies. Amount: up to full costs. www.indiana.edu

Kansas State University. General scholarship deadline. Criteria and amounts vary. www.ksu.edu

Miami University (OH). Harrison Scholars. Criteria: all-around excellence. Amount: up to the full costs of attendance. www.muohio.edu

University of Michigan. General scholarship priority deadline. Criteria: varies. Amount: up to $10,000. www.umich.edu

Michigan State University. Alumni Distinguished Scholarships. Criteria: academic excellence. Amount: up to the full costs of attendance. www.msu.edu

North Carolina State University. Park Scholarship. Criteria: all-around excellence. Amount: up to the full costs of attendance. School nomination required where applicable. www.ncsu.edu

Scripps College. James E. Scripps Scholarships. Criteria: all-around excellence. Amount: half of tuition. www.scrippscollege.edu

University of Tennessee. General scholarship deadline. Criteria and amounts vary. www.utk.edu

Villanova University. Presidential Scholarship. Criteria: 3.8 GPA and 1400 SAT or 32 ACT. Amount: full tuition. www.villanova.edu

University of Virginia. Jefferson Scholars Nomination. Criteria: all-around excellence. Amount: up to full costs of attendance and summer stipend. School nomination required where applicable. www.jeffersonscholars.org

Washington University in St. Louis. Danforth Scholars. Criteria: all-around excellence. Amount: up to full tuition. School nomination required. www.wustl.edu

November 10
University of North Carolina at Asheville. University Laurels Scholarships. Criteria: 3.5 GPA and 1250 SAT or 28 ACT. Amount: up to the full costs of attendance. www.unca.edu

November 15
DePaul University. General scholarship deadline. Criteria: varies. Amount: up to $13,000. www.depaul.edu

University of Georgia. Foundation Fellows. Criteria: 1400 SAT or 31 ACT. Amount: up to $14,000. www.uga.edu

Louisiana State University. General scholarship deadline. Criteria: varies. Amount: up to $3,000. www.lsu.edu

University of San Francisco. University Scholars. Criteria: 3.8 GPA and 1320 SAT or 30 ACT. Amount: $16,000. www.usfca.edu

December 1
University of Alabama. General scholarship deadline. Criteria: academic excellence. Amount: varies. www.ua.edu

Auburn University. General scholarship deadline. Criteria: academic excellence. Amount: up to $10,500. www.auburn.edu.

Boston University. Trustee Scholarship. Criteria: all-around excellence. Amount: full tuition. School nomination required. www.bu.edu

Butler University. Departmental Scholarships. Criteria: varies. Amount: $2,000–$3,000. www.butler.edu

University of Connecticut. General scholarship deadline. Criteria: varies. Amount: up to $9,800. www.uconn.edu

Fairfield University. General scholarship deadline. Criteria: varies. Amount: up to $16,000. www.fairfield.edu

Loyola University New Orleans. General scholarship deadline. Criteria: academic excellence, artistic talent. Amount: up to $14,000. www.loyno.edu

University of Maryland at College Park. General scholarship deadline. Criteria and amounts vary. www.umd.edu

University of Missouri at Columbia. General scholarship deadline. Criteria: varies. Amount: $7,500. www.missouri.edu

University of Missouri at Rolla. General scholarship deadline. Criteria: academic excellence. Amount: varies. www.umr.edu

University of New Mexico. Regents and Presidential Scholarships. Criteria: academic excellence. Amount: Up to the full costs of attendance. www.unm.edu

Purdue University. Beering School of Science Scholarships (by invitation only). Criteria and amounts vary. www.purdue.edu

Rutgers–The State University of New Jersey. General scholarship deadline. Criteria: varies. Amount: up to $15,000. www.rutgers.edu

University of South Carolina. General scholarship deadline. Criteria: academic excellence. Amount: up to $12,000. www.sc.edu

St. Louis University. General scholarship deadline. Criteria: varies. Amount: up to full tuition. www.slu.edu

University of Texas at Austin. General scholarship deadline. Criteria and amounts vary. www.utexas.edu

Wake Forest University. Reynolds Scholarships. Criteria: all-around excellence. Amount: full costs of attendance and summer stipend. www.wfu.edu

December 1
Ohio State University. University Scholar Maximus Scholarships. Criteria: varies. Amount: up to the full costs of attendance. www.osu.edu

December 5
Oglethorpe College. JEO Scholarship. Criteria: 3.75 GPA and 1360 SAT or 31 ACT. Amount: full costs of attendance. www.oglethorpe.edu

Presbyterian College. General scholarship deadline. Criteria: varies. Amount: up to full costs of attendance. www.presbyterian.edu

December 10
Randolph College. Presidential Scholarships. Criteria: all-around excellence. Amount: up to the full costs of attendance with travel stipend. www.rmwc.edu

University of Southern California. General scholarship deadline. Criteria: varies. Amount: up to full tuition. www.usc.edu

December 15
University of Iowa. Presidential and Dean's Scholarships. Criteria: academic excellence. Amount: $7,000 and $1,000, respectively. www.uiowa.edu

Ithaca College. Park Scholarship in journalism and communications. Criteria: top 5 percent and 1300 SAT. Amount: up to the full costs of attendance. www.ithaca.edu

Kenyon College. Honor and Science Scholarships. Criteria: varies. Amount: up to half tuition. www.kenyon.edu

University of Redlands. General scholarship deadline. Criteria: varies. Amount: from $500 to $10,000. www.redlands.edu

University of Rhode Island. Centennial Scholarships. Criteria: Class rank in top third and 1150 SAT or 25 ACT. Amount: up to full tuition. www.uri.edu

University of Richmond. Oldham Scholarship and Ethyl and Albemarle Science Scholarship. Criteria: all-around excellence. Amount: Full costs of attendance and summer stipend. www.richmond.edu

Tulane University. Dean's Honor Scholarship. Criteria: 1450 SAT I or 33 ACT. Amount: full tuition. www.tulane.edu

Wabash College. President's Scholarships. Criteria: class rank top 20 percent and 1150 SAT or 25 ACT. Amount: $2,500-$12,500. www.wabash.edu

Washington & Lee University. George Washington Honor Scholarship. Criteria: all-around excellence. Amount: up to the full costs of attendance. www.wlu.edu

December 31

Clemson University. General scholarship deadline. Criteria and amounts vary. www.clemson.edu

University of North Carolina at Chapel Hill. Pogue Scholarships. Criteria: All-around excellence, special emphasis on minority applicants. Amount: $7,500. www.unc.edu

January 8

Millsaps College. Presidential and Second Century Scholarships. Criteria: all-around excellence. Amount: up to $25,000. www.millsaps.edu

January 15

Rhodes College. Bellingrath Scholarship Nomination. Criteria: all-around excellence. Amount: up to the full costs of attendance. Nomination required. www.rhodes.edu

February 1

University of Oklahoma. General scholarship deadline. Some scholarships awarded as early as November. Criteria and amounts vary. www.ou.edu

GLOSSARY

The language of college admission is replete with arcane acronyms and obscure terms. Here are some definitions.

ACT: A nonprofit organization that administers the standardized test that bears its name. Most colleges allow students to submit results from either the ACT or the SAT to satisfy the standardized testing requirement. ACT is not affiliated with the College Board or ETS.

Advanced Placement (AP): Courses taught under the aegis of the College Board Advanced Placement Program. These courses follow a standard curriculum and culminate in exams scored on a scale of 1–5. High scores qualify students for credit at participating colleges.

College Board: Also known as the College Entrance Examination Board, the College Board produces the Preliminary SAT (PSAT), the SAT, and the Subject Tests. The College Board also runs the Advanced Placement (AP) Program and one of its subdivisions, the College Scholarship Service, is the maker of the CSS/Financial Aid PROFILE. See also: Educational Testing Service.

Common Application: A standard application form that is accepted by more than two hundred selective colleges in lieu of their own form. Available at www.commonapp.org and in high school guidance offices.

consortium: A group of colleges or universities that offer joint programs or allow students from one institution to take courses at another.

CSS/Financial Aid PROFILE: A financial aid form produced by the College Board that is required for students seeking aid at approximately 10 percent of the nation's four-year colleges (including most highly selective institutions).

deferral: The term applied to applications for early action or early decision that are deferred for consideration with the regular application pool.

demonstrated need: The difference between the Expected Family Contribution (EFC) and the total cost of attendance at a particular institution.

early action (EA): A program whereby students receive an early-admission decision, but are not obligated to enroll if admitted. Also known as early notification.

early decision (ED): A program that gives students an early admission decision with the obligation to enroll if admitted and to withdraw applications from other institutions.

Educational Testing Service (ETS): A nonprofit organization that designs and administers the SAT I and II through a contractual arrangement with the College Board.

federal methodology (FM): The method of calculating the Expected Family Contribution (EFC) that rests solely on the data submitted in the Free Application for Federal Student Aid (FAFSA) and the federal aid formula.

financial aid package: The bundle of aid awarded by a particular college that may include grants, loans, and a work-study job.

Free Application for Federal Student Aid (FAFSA): A financial aid form produced by the federal government that is required for students seeking aid by nearly all colleges and universities.

institutional methodology (IM): A method of calculating Expected Family Contribution (EFC) that varies by college and may depend on data submitted in the Free Application for Federal Student Aid (FAFSA), the CSS/Financial Aid PROFILE, and the college's own aid form.

institutional scholarship: A scholarship awarded by a college or university. Generally available only to students who plan to enroll.

International Baccalaureate (IB): A program offered by schools in more than one hundred nations that covers six academic areas in the final two years of high school, culminating in an IB diploma. In the U.S., participation in IB is relatively small compared to AP.

National Merit Scholarship Program: A scholarship and recognition program based primarily on scores from the Preliminary SAT (PSAT). More than 7,500 students each year receive scholarships based on National Merit status, ranging from several hundred dollars to the full costs of attendance. Separate programs honor African American and Hispanic students.

need-blind admission: The term that applies to colleges that make admission decisions without regard to the financial circumstances of the applicants. Colleges with need-blind admission do not necessarily offer aid to meet the full need of all accepted applicants.

PLAN: A test produced by ACT that is administered by schools in the fall of 10th grade. PLAN can help predict ACT scores.

preferential packaging: A method of awarding financial aid in which colleges offer the best aid packages to their most desired applicants.

Preliminary SAT (PSAT): A test produced by the College Board that is administered by high schools to 11th graders and some 10th graders. The PSAT is the qualifying test for consideration in the National Merit Scholarship Program.

Reserve Officer Training Corps (ROTC): A program that offers scholarships up to full tuition at hundreds of colleges nationwide. Students earn a degree while training part-time for military service. After graduation, students are generally required to serve on active duty for four years. Offered by the Army, Navy, and Air Force.

rolling admission: The term describing admission without fixed application deadlines. Applications are evaluated as they are received until the class is full.

SAT and Subject Tests: Formerly known as SAT I, the SAT is a three-hour test that consists of verbal and math sections. The Subject Tests, formerly known as SAT IIs and Achievement Tests, are one-hour tests devoted to particular subjects.

self-help: A term that describes the portion of a financial aid package consisting of loans and wages from a work-study job.

Student Aid Report (SAR): A form sent to families in response to submission of the Free Application for Federal Student Aid (FAFSA) that includes the Expected Family Contribution (EFC), a figure that may be modified at colleges that use institutional methodology (IM).

wait list (or waitlist): A list of applicants to a particular college who are not admitted in the regular-decision pool, but who may be considered if space is still available after admitted students have indicated whether or not they will attend.

work study: A federally funded program wherein students are given campus jobs with the wages calculated as part of their financial aid package.

yield: The percentage of accepted applicants at a particular college who choose to enroll.

ACKNOWLEDGMENTS

We are grateful to many people who assisted in the publication of this book. The members of the Fiske College Counselors Advisory Group, listed below, provided important input. They were our source for the "Counselor's heads-up" advice, and students and parents from their school communities are also quoted in the text.

We are grateful to Laura Johnson Frey for her thorough reading of the first edition of the book. Mary Anne Modzelewski, Bruce's colleague at Sandia Preparatory School, has been an important source of support, as was Julie Fiske Hogan, production coordinator of the *Fiske Guide to Colleges*. Cheryl Davis, Guy Hammond, and Jean Hammond also provided valuable editing assistance.

We are deeply indebted to our editors at Sourcebooks, including Todd Stocke, Peter Lynch, and Erin Nevius, whose enthusiasm for and dedication to the Fiske guides have been an inspiration. Also, thanks to Matt Diamond for his hard work on the design of this book.

College Counselors Advisory Group

Marilyn Albarelli, Moravian Academy (PA)
Scott Anderson, St. George's Independent School (TN)
Christine Asmussen, St. Andrew's-Sewanee School (TN)
Bruce Bailey, Lakeside School (WA)
Amy E. Belstra, Cherry Creek H.S. (CO)
Greg Birk, Kinkaid School (TX)
Susan T. Bisson, Advocates for Human Potential (MA)
Francine E. Block, American College Admissions
     Consultants (PA)
Robin Boren, Education Consultant (CO)
Clarice Boring, Cody H.S. (WY)
John B. Boshoven, Community High School &
     Jewish Academy of Metro Detroit (MI)
Mimi Bradley, St. Andrew's Episcopal School (MS)
Claire Cafaro, Clear Directions (NJ)
Nancy Caine, St. Augustine H.S. (CA)
Jane M. Catanzaro, College Advising Services (CT)
Mary Chapman, St. Catherine's School (VA)
Anthony L. Clay, Durham Academy (NC)

Kathy Cleaver, Durham Academy (NC)
Jimmie Lee Cogburn, Independent Counselor (GA)
Alison Cotten, Cypress Falls H.S. (TX)
Alice Cotti, Polytechnic School (CA)
Rod Cox, St. Johns Country Day School (FL)
Kim Crockard, Crockard College Counseling (AL)
Carroll K. Davis, North Central H.S. (IN)
Mary Jo Dawson, Academy of the Sacred Heart (MI)
Christy Dillon, Crystal Springs Uplands School (CA)
Lexi Eagles, Greensboro Country Day School (NC)
Dan Feldhaus, Iolani School (HI)
Ralph S. Figueroa, Albuquerque Academy (NM)
Emily E. FitzHugh, The Gunnery (CT)
Mary Fitzsimmons, Fiske Guide Workshops (NJ)
Larry Fletcher, Salesianum School (DE)
Nancy Fomby, Episcopal School of Dallas (TX)
Daniel Franklin, Education Consultant (CO)
Laura Johnson Frey, Vermont Academy (VT)
Phyllis Gill, Providence Day School (NC)
H. Scotte Gordon, Moses Brown School (RI)

Freida Gottsegen, Education Consultant (GA)
Molly Gotwals, Suffield Academy (CT)
Kathleen Barnes Grant, The Catlin Gabel School (OR)
Madelyn Gray, John Burroughs School (MO)
Amy Grieger, Northfield Mount Hermon School (MA)
Mimi Grossman, St. Mary's Episcopal School (TN)
Elizabeth Hall, Education Consulting Services (TX)
Andrea L. Hays, Education Consultant (GA)
Darnell Heywood, Columbus School for Girls (OH)
Bruce Hunter, Rowland Hall-St. Mark's School (UT)
Deanna L. Hunter, Shawnee Mission East H.S. (KS)
John Keyes, The Catlin Gabel School (OR)
Linda King, College Connections (NY)
Sharon Koenings, Brookfield Academy (WI)
Joan Jacobson, Shawnee Mission South H.S. (KS)
Diane Johnson, Lawrence Public Schools (NY)
Gerimae Kleinman, Shaker Heights H.S. (OH)
Laurie Leftwich, Brother Martin High School (LA)
MaryJane London, Los Angeles Center for Enriched Studies (CA)
Martha Lyman, Deerfield Academy (MA)
Brad MacGowan, Newton North H.S. (MA)
Robert S. MacLellan, Jr., Hebron Academy (ME)
Margaret M. Man, La Pietra-Hawaii School for Girls (HI)
Susan Marrs, The Seven Hills School (OH)

Karen A. Mason, Wyoming Seminary (PA)
Lynne McConnell, Rumson-Fair Haven Regional H.S. (NJ)
Lisa Micele, University of Illinois Laboratory H.S. (IL)
Corky Miller-Strong, The Culver Academies (IN)
Janet Miranda, Prestonwood Christian Academy (TX)
Joyce Vining Morgan, White Mountain School (NH)
Daniel Murphy, The Urban School of San Francisco (CA)
Judith Nash, Highland High School (ID)
Gunnar W. Olson, Indian Springs School (AL)
Stuart Oremus, Wellington School (OH)
Deborah Robinson, Mandarin H.S. (FL)
Julie Rollins, Episcopal H.S. (TX)
William C. Rowe, Thomas Jefferson School (MO)
Bruce Scher, Chicagoland Jewish H.S. (IL)
David Schindel, Sandia Preparatory School (NM)
Kathy Z. Schmidt, St. Mary's Hall (TX)
Barbara Simmons, Notre Dame High School (CA)
Joe Stehno, Bishop Brady H.S. (NH)
Bruce Stempien, Weston H.S. (CT)
Paul M. Stoneham, The Key School (MD)
Ted de Villafranca, Peddie School (NJ)
Scott White, Montclair H.S. (NJ)
Linda Zimring, Los Angeles United School District (CA)

JANUARY 2008

S	M	T	W	T	F	S
		1	2	3	4	5
6	7	8	9	10	11	12
13	14	15	16	17	18	19
20	21	22	23	24	25	26
27	28	29	30	31		

FEBRUARY 2008

S	M	T	W	T	F	S
					1	2
3	4	5	6	7	8	9
10	11	12	13	14	15	16
17	18	19	20	21	22	23
24	25	26	27	28	29	

MARCH 2008

S	M	T	W	T	F	S
						1
2	3	4	5	6	7	8
9	10	11	12	13	14	15
16	17	18	19	20	21	22
23	24	25	26	27	28	29
30	31					

APRIL 2008

S	M	T	W	T	F	S
		1	2	3	4	5
6	7	8	9	10	11	12
13	14	15	16	17	18	19
20	21	22	23	24	25	26
27	28	29	30			

MAY 2008

S	M	T	W	T	F	S
				1	2	3
4	5	6	7	8	9	10
11	12	13	14	15	16	17
18	19	20	21	22	23	24
25	26	27	28	29	30	31

JUNE 2008

S	M	T	W	T	F	S
1	2	3	4	5	6	7
8	9	10	11	12	13	14
15	16	17	18	19	20	21
22	23	24	25	26	27	28
29	30					

JULY 2008

S	M	T	W	T	F	S
		1	2	3	4	5
6	7	8	9	10	11	12
13	14	15	16	17	18	19
20	21	22	23	24	25	26
27	28	29	30	31		

AUGUST 2008

S	M	T	W	T	F	S
					1	2
3	4	5	6	7	8	9
10	11	12	13	14	15	16
17	18	19	20	21	22	23
24	25	26	27	28	29	30
31						

SEPTEMBER 2008

S	M	T	W	T	F	S
	1	2	3	4	5	6
7	8	9	10	11	12	13
14	15	16	17	18	19	20
21	22	23	24	25	26	27
28	29	30				

OCTOBER 2008

S	M	T	W	T	F	S
			1	2	3	4
5	6	7	8	9	10	11
12	13	14	15	16	17	18
19	20	21	22	23	24	25
26	27	28	29	30	31	

NOVEMBER 2008

S	M	T	W	T	F	S
						1
2	3	4	5	6	7	8
9	10	11	12	13	14	15
16	17	18	19	20	21	22
23	24	25	26	27	28	29
30						

DECEMBER 2008

S	M	T	W	T	F	S
	1	2	3	4	5	6
7	8	9	10	11	12	13
14	15	16	17	18	19	20
21	22	23	24	25	26	27
28	29	30	31			

JANUARY 2009

S	M	T	W	T	F	S
				1	2	3
4	5	6	7	8	9	10
11	12	13	14	15	16	17
18	19	20	21	22	23	24
25	26	27	28	29	30	31

FEBRUARY 2009

S	M	T	W	T	F	S
1	2	3	4	5	6	7
8	9	10	11	12	13	14
15	16	17	18	19	20	21
22	23	24	25	26	27	28

MARCH 2009

S	M	T	W	T	F	S
1	2	3	4	5	6	7
8	9	10	11	12	13	14
15	16	17	18	19	20	21
22	23	24	25	26	27	28
29	30	31				

APRIL 2009

S	M	T	W	T	F	S
			1	2	3	4
5	6	7	8	9	10	11
12	13	14	15	16	17	18
19	20	21	22	23	24	25
26	27	28	29	30		

NOTES

NOTES

NOTES

NOTES

NOTES

NOTES

NOTES

NOTES

NOTES

NOTES

NOTES

NOTES

DON'T MISS THOSE DEADLINES!

VISIT

SOURCEBOOKSCOLLEGE.COM

AND SIGN UP FOR EMAIL UPDATES

ON ALL THE TESTING, ADMISSIONS

AND SCHOLARSHIP DEADLINES YOU

NEED TO KNOW.

BROUGHT TO YOU BY

EDWARD B. FISKE AND BRUCE G. HAMMOND